Cool Names
for Babies

Pamela Redmond Satran
and
Linda Rosenkrantz

HarperCollins*Publishers*
77–85 Fulham Palace Road
Hammersmith
London W6 8JB

The Collins website address is www.collins.co.uk

First published in the USA in 2003 by St Martin's Press
First published in the UK in 2004 by Collins
This edition published in 2006
Collins is a registered trademark of HarperCollins Publishers Ltd

9

**A catalogue record for this book is available
from the British Library**

ISBN 13: 978-0-00-718057-8
ISBN 10: 0-00-718057-8

This   d
fro

Print

Cool Names
for Babies

Collins

Contents

II. COOL COOL — *Famous Names* · 49

III. PRE-COOL COOL — *Old Names* · 107

IV. NEW COOL — Creative Names · 131

Introduction

We got the idea for this book when we were doing publicity for our last book on names, *Baby Names Now*. One after another, interviewers seemed to ask us the same question, 'What are the cool names?' And each time, we found ourselves stumped.

Since we wrote our first book together, *Beyond Jennifer & Jason* (now amended to *Beyond Jennifer & Jason, Madison & Montana*), we've broken down names into the trendy and the classic, the feminine and the androgynous, into categories ranging from Irish to unusual, from Shakespeare to soap opera. Over 15 years of updates to that book, we'd classified names every way possible except one. We'd never examined precisely what makes a name cool, and which names fit the bill. Of course, we'd spent the last 15 years thinking about cool names. . . .

And that's the big question today, after all, the thing that most parents – along with those persistent interviewers – want to know. What are the cool names? And how can I choose one for my child?

In examining the issue of cool and names, we reached a few conclusions.

Cool, for the Most Part, Means Unusual.

Cool names today usually are those that are not familiar. Traditional choices like John and Elizabeth (this is undoubtedly the only name book on the market that does not include the names John and Elizabeth) are simply too normal to be considered cool. And popular favourites like Oscar and Ella are too widespread to be cool. Now that the Top 10 names include such once-wild choices as Chloe and Joshua, you have to go pretty far beyond the mainstream to find names that are truly cool.

Cool Knows No Boundaries.

All names from all cultures are fair game for parents in search of cool these days – as well as surnames, place names, nature and day names, transgender names, and word names. And why stop there? In this book, we offer up some new categories no one ever thought of before: foreign-word names, for instance, like Vrai.

If You Can't Find a Cool Name You Like, Make One Up.

Unusual doesn't go far enough for some parents: they want a name that's truly one-of-a-kind. Parents in search of a cool name are more often creating one of their own, and we include here advice on how to do that. Our only caveat: if you want a name that's truly cool, be creative in your invention and don't make a very minor alteration to a very popular name.

There's Plenty of Inspiration Out There for Cool.

The world is full of inspiration for cool baby-naming – and more full every day, thanks to the cool names of characters in films and books and to the names of celebrities themselves. Plus, with last names now as fair game as first names, the pool of famous names virtually doubles – Madonna and Cher notwithstanding.

Kids Today Are Comfortable with Cool.

When we were growing up, if you had a name like Sonata or Sawyer, other children thought you were weird. But now that the concept of cool permeates the culture, down to children's own ideas about desirability, kids take unusual names in their stride and even admire them. Our own children's friends include an Ash and a Dash, a (girl) Baldwin, a Miles and an Allegra and a Lex and a Xan, and they don't even blink. So if the only thing that's stopping you from choosing a cooler name is worrying about how your child will handle it, don't.

There Are Many Kinds of Cool.

A cool name can be an invented one – or a name from the Bible such as Moses or Tabitha that's fallen out of favour. It can be an androgynous choice like O'Hara, or a name with clear gender associations: Felicity, say, or Finn. Cool names include the earthly (Tierra) and the otherworldly (Jupiter), the ancient (Abel) and the newly minted (Arley). You can find a cool name to suit any sensibility.

Cool Isn't Everything.

Along with many varieties, there are several levels of cool, from the Hot – these are popular names such as Isabella and Isaiah that are widely considered cool – to the Over-the-Top. How far you want to go depends on your taste, your sense of adventure, and where you live. One Manhattan-based parent we know, for instance, recently rejected the name Oscar as 'too common' – though in most parts of the US, Oscar is too cool for consideration. So what if you're one of those people who realize you don't want to go even halfway to Oscar? What if you read this book and find yourself intrigued, entertained, inspired . . . and in the end a lot more convinced than you realized that you want to give your child a plain, solid, and decidedly uncool name like John or Elizabeth?

So what indeed. A name is not your personal style statement, a choice with which to impress the world. Rather, you should think of it as something that will identify your child for the rest of their life, a label they will have to live with forever. You may decide that cool is a desirable component of such a lifelong imprimatur. And then again, you may decide that, when it comes to a name, you want nothing to do with cool (just know you well may have to suffer the consequences when your child is a teenager).

And that's fine. But you still owe it to your baby and your choice of a name to read this book. For one thing, we offer hundreds and hundreds of naming options here that you won't find ANYWHERE else. We'll open your eyes to a way of thinking about names that no other book, no other source can. And you'll know for certain, after reading this book, what makes for a cool name – even if you decide that uncool is cool enough for you.

I. HOT COOL

...

Mainstream Names

Callum

The Top 20 of Cool

What's cool and what's popular is often decidedly *not* the same thing. But as the taste for cool becomes more widespread, as offbeat names continue to supplant stalwarts such as John and Mary on the popularity lists, we are finding more crossover between those names considered cool and those that make the top of the pops.

This list is the Top 20 Cool Names drawn from the most recent compilation of 100 Most Popular Names in England and Wales. They're ranked in order of frequency, so that Lily is not necessarily the coolest name of the group, but it is the name given to the most girls in that year. The number in brackets indicates each name's rank on the overall popularity list.

Depending on your personal tolerance for cool, you may see the names here as either outrageous or a bit dull. In either case, for first-time parents this list may be an eye-opening look at just how popular these choices are. And for those who want to find a name that's cool without being unique or unusual or wild, the names on this list can offer a good compromise.

But cool is a subjective quality, and while we've selected 20 of what we think are the coolest names, you may find others in the larger group you consider cooler. If you want to consult the overall popularity lists for the UK as well as several other European countries and the US, one good source is the website behindthename.com.

Girls

1. **AMELIA** (14)
2. **LILY** (16)
3. **MIA** (18)
4. **MILLIE** (20)
5. **DAISY** (28)
6. **PHOEBE** (35)
7. **KEIRA** (38)
8. **POPPY** (39)
9. **ALICE** (44)
10. **SCARLETT** (47)
11. **LIBBY** (48)
12. **NIAMH** (50)
13. **MAISIE** (55)
14. **EVE** (58)
15. **ROSIE** (61)
16. **SIENNA** (69)
17. **AVA** (84)
18. **GRACIE** (87)
19. **LOLA** (93)
20. **TILLY** (95)

Boys

1. **CALLUM** (15)	11. **OSCAR** (54)
2. **JAKE** (16)	12. **FINLAY** (57)
3. **GEORGE** (18)	13. **RHYS** (59)
4. **ALFIE** (22)	14. **MASON** (62)
5. **HARVEY** (27)	15. **JOE** (63)
6. **OWEN** (36)	16. **KAI** (67)
7. **ARCHIE** (38)	17. **HARLEY** (72)
8. **LOUIS** (42)	18. **LUCA** (83)
9. **TOBY** (48)	19. **EWAN** (89)
10. **KIERAN** (49)	20. **ZAK** (99)

CELTIC COOL

The popularity lists of Ireland and, to some extent, Scotland, are crowded with Celtic names that are beginning to win widespread acceptance as cool names. A few are included above. Here are other cool Celtic choices that appear on popularity lists. For help with pronunciation of the Irish selections, go to babynamesofireland.com, where you can hear Frank McCourt, author of *Angela's Ashes*, say each name.

Girls

AINE	**CAOIMHE**
AISLING	**CLODAGH**
AOIBHE	
	EABHA
AOIFE	
	EIMEAR

GRAINNE

MAEVE

NIAMH

ORLA

ORLAITH

ROISIN

SADHBH

SAORISE

SIOBHAN

Boys

CATHAL

CIAN/KIAN

CIARRAN

CILLIAN/KILLIAN

COLM

DAIRE

DARA/DARAGH/
   DARRAGH

DIARMUID

EOGHAN

EOIN

FINN

FIONN

LORCAN

NIALL

ODHRAN

OISIN

ORAN

PADRAIGH

RIAN

RONAN

RORY

TADHG

DOWN UNDER COOL

What's cool in Australia and New Zealand is a bit similar to what's cool in the British Isles, a bit like what's cool in the

US – and a bit like nothing else at all. Here are some cool names Down Under:

Girls

ABBEY	JASMINE	RUBY
AMELIE	JORJA	SCARLETT
AVA		SIENNA
	KIARA	
CHARLI		SKYE
CHARLIZE	LILY	
		TAHLIA
	MIA	
ELIZA	MOLLY	TAYLA
		TIA
IMOGEN		
	PARIS	ZARA
	PHOEBE	

Boys

ANGUS	ETHAN	LACHLAN
ASHTON		LUCA
	FLYNN	
BLAKE		OSCAR
BRAYDEN	HAMISH	OWEN
BROCK	HARRISON	
BRODIE	HUDSON	RILEY
	JAXON	TYSON
CHARLIE	JAYDEN	
COOPER	JETT	XAVIER
DECLAN		ZAC
DYLAN	KAI	

Polly Dolly Molly

Coolator

O ften, it doesn't take much to change the cool status of a name. For many girls' names, all you have to do, figuratively, is add an 'a' to the end to bump them up several coolness levels: Lucy to Lucia, Helen to Helena – you get the picture. The point is that with a bit of ingenuity you can ramp up a name you like to a similar one that's cooler, or tone it down if you want to go in a quieter direction. Here are some examples:

Girls

UNCOOL	COOL	COOLER
ANNE	ANNA	ANYA
BRENDA	BRONWYN	BRYONY
CAROL	CAROLINE	CAROLINA
CHARMAINE	CHARLOTTE	CARLOTTA
CINDY	SYDNEY	SIDONIE
CRYSTAL	JADE	RUBY
DAWN	AURORA	ANDROMEDA
DIANE	DIANA	DINAH
EILEEN	ELLEN	ELENA
EVELYN	EVE	AVA
GEORGINA	GEORGIA	GEORGIANA
GWEN	GWYNNE	GWYNETH
HEATHER	DAISY	VIOLET
HELEN	HELENE	HELENA
JAMIE	JAMESON	JAMAICA
JAN	JANNA	JANICA
JEANETTE	JEMIMA	JENNA
JENNIFER	GENEVIEVE	GENEVA
JOAN	JOLIE	JOSEPHINE
JUNE	JUNO	JUNIPER
LAURA	NORA	DORA
LILIAN	LILY	LILO

LISA	LIZA	ELIZA
LORRAINE	LAUREL	LAURENCE
LUCY	LULU	LUCIA
MARIE	MARIA	MIREILLE
MARY	MERCY	MURRAY
PATRICIA	PATRIZIA	PATIENCE
POLLY	DOLLY	MOLLY
ROSEMARY	SAGE	SAFFRON
SAMANTHA	SAMARA	SASKIA
SERENA	SELENA	SERAFINA
STACY	LACEY	MACY
STEPHANIE	STELLA	STORY
TAMMY	TAMARA	TAMAR
ZOE	ZORA	ZOLA

Boys

UNCOOL	COOL	COOLER
ADRIAN	AIDAN	ADLAI
ALAN	ALCOTT	ALDO
ARNOLD	ARNE	ARNO
ASHLEY	ASHER	ASH
BILL	WILL	WILLEM
BRUCE	BRYCE	BRUNO
CHARLES	CHARLIE	CARLO
CRAIG	CRISPIN	CROSBY
DARRYL	DARIUS	DASHIELL

UNCOOL	COOL	COOLER
DAVE	DAVIS	DAMON
EDDIE	EDWARD	NED
GEOFF	JEB	JEX
HENRY	HARRY	HARDY
IAN	IVOR	INIGO
JAMIE	JAMESON	JAGO
JOHN	JACK	GIACOMO
KEN	SVEN	XEN
KENNETH	KENT	KENYON
LEE	LEO	LEONARDO
MIKE	MAC	MAGUIRE
MORRIS	MORGAN	MORRISON
RAYMOND	RAY	RAOUL
RONALD	RONAN	ROAN
WAYNE	KANE	ZANE

Dakota

American Names

The coolest American names are not names at all, at least not conventional first names that have ever been used for people. Rather, they're invented names, place names, surnames, word names. And, for better and worse, they're poised to enter the culture of countries beyond the United States, as surely as The Gap and Coca-Cola.

The hottest of these – invented names commonly thought of as 'American' in the least flattering sense – have rapidly climbed the popularity list in the US over the past decade and are already booming in Australia. Still rarely heard in the UK, but shouted from every street corner from Boston to LA, are such trendies as:

Girls

ADDISON

AINSLEY

ARIA

ASHTON

AUBREY

AUTUMN

AVERY

BROOKLYN

BRYN

CADENCE

CALI

CAMERON

CAMPBELL

CASSIDY

CHANEL

CHEYENNE

DANIA

DELANEY

DESTINY

ELLE

EMERSON

ESSENCE

GENESIS

HARLEY

HARMONY

HAVEN

HEAVEN

JADEN

JORDAN

JUSTICE

KALYN

KENNEDY

LEXI

LIBERTY

LOGAN

MACY

MADISON

MCKENNA

MCKENZIE

NEVAEH

PEYTON

PRESLEY

QUINN   SKYLAR

RAVEN   TRINITY
RYLIE   TRISTA

SKYLA   WILLOW
SKYE

Boys

BLAINE   COOPER
BLAZE   CORBIN
BRADEN   CORTEZ
BRANSON
BRAXTON   DAKOTA
BRODY   DALLIN
BRYSON   DALTON
               DANE
CADEN   DARWIN
CALE   DAYTON
CANNON   DEACON
CARSON   DRAKE
CLAY
CLAYTON   EASTON
CODY   EFREN
COLBY
COLE   FISHER
COLTON

GAGE

GANNON

GRADY

GRAYSON

HUDSON

HUNTER

JADEN

JAMESON

JAYLEN

KAI

KEEGAN

KELLEN

KENYON

KIAN

KYLAN

KYLER

LANDON

LANE

LINCOLN

LOGAN

MAVERICK

PARKER

REAGAN

REID

REMINGTON

RIVER

RYDER

RYKER

RYLAN

RYLAND

SAGE

SAWYER

STONE

SULLIVAN

TATE

TEAGAN

TRACE

TRENTON

WADE

WESTON

WYATT

Tanguy

Foreign Names

Foreign names is another of those categories that is vast and almost uniformly cool, at least to the unschooled ear (and we'd include our own in that category) – but beyond the reach of this book. For further selections, see our *Beyond Jennifer & Jason, Madison & Montana* as well as *Baby Names Now*, or search the internet for name sites overseas (try to find the real ones, not some American listing of Italian or French names – which often is incomplete and doesn't include the really interesting foreign choices). There are also a lot of foreign names sprinkled throughout this book. This group consists of those that didn't fit into any of our other categories and that we think are especially appealing and, yes, cool.

Girls

ALEXANE

ANIKA

ANJA

ANTONELLA

ARIELA

AVELINA

AZIZA

BENICIA

BRIGITTE

CALANDRA

CALLA

CARMEN

CHANTAL

COSIMA

DANICA

DELPHINE

ELEA

ELETTRA

ELIANA

ELISKA

ÉLODIE

ENORA

ESTELLA

FEDERICA

FERNANDA

FIA

FRANCESCA

FYODORA

GELSEY

GIANNA

GIOIA

GRAZIANA

GRAZIELLA

GRETA

GUADALUPE

IMAN

INEZ

INGRID

IRINA

IRINI

JANICA

JOZEFINA

KALILA

KALINDI

KATYA

LAILA/LAYLA/

LEILA

LARISA

LUDMILA	RAFFAELA/
LUDOVICA	RAPHAELA
LUPE	RENATA
MALIA	SANDRINE
MANON	SANNE
MANUELA	SARITA
MARCELLA	SASKIA
MARINA	SAVITA
MARINE	SÉVERINE
MARIT	SIDRA
MIGNON	SIMONE
	SIRI
NADYA	SOLANGE
NATALYA	SYBILLA
NIAMH (pron. Neev)	SYLVIE/SILVIE
PAOLA	TATIANA
PERDITA	
PETRA	YELENA
PIA	ZUZANNA

Boys

ALEXEI	BAPTISTE
ANATOLI	
ANDREAS	CORENTIN
ANSELMO	CYR
ARMANDO	DIMITRI

ELIAN

ELIO

ERASMO

ÉTIENNE

FLANN

FLYNN

FRITZ

FYODOR

GASTON

GIANNI

GRADY

GUIDO

GUILLAUME

GUSTAF

HELIO

ILYA

IVAN

JANOS

KAZIMIR

KRISTOF

LAURENT

LEOPOLD

LUC

LUCIEN

MALO

MAREK

MATEO

MIGUEL

MIKHAIL

MIKOLAS

NICASIO

NIKO

PABLO

PAOLO

PER

PIER

RAMON

RAOUL

SERGEI

TADDEO

TANGUY

TIBOR

TOMASZ

VASILI

VLADIMIR

WOLF

UMBERTO

ZOLTAN

Luca

What Europeans Call Cool

Ask young European parents what names they think
are cool, and you are in for a real education. The
ultimate lesson is that taste in names is culturally specific and
unpredictable. Consider these reports:

ITALY

Our friend and informal correspondent Claudio Aspesi
reports that, among upper-middle-class Milanese parents,
traditional and aristocratic names – some of them with an

Old German or Russian flavour – are coming back into style. These include:

Girls	Boys
ALLEGRA	FILIPPO
BEATRICE	FRANCESCO
BIANCA MARIA	GIOVANNI
CAROLINA	LORENZO
DESIDERIA	NICOLO
DOMITILLA	TANCREDI
FEDERICA	TOMMASO
FRANCESCA	
GIORGIA	
LUDOVICA	
MARIA	
MARTINA	

GERMANY

The number one boy's name in Germany right now is Leon. Interestingly, Leon has become almost a joke in the US because it's so popular but it in fact has a noble history as the Greek form (Leo is the Latin) for 'lion'. From Germany, Anja Toepper reports that classical names – as opposed to 'American' choices – are coming back into favour. But there's a big difference between cool classical and old-fashioned names that, Toepper says, 'would mean a punishment for a kid'. If you want to find a German name for your child, avoid these traditional but highly uncool choices: for girls, Gerda, Gertrud, Hannelore, Hedwig, Elke, Ilse; and, for boys, Wilhelm, Heinz, Egon, Erwin, Franz, Jürgen, Hermann, Horst, Dietrich, Manfred, Gerhard, Kurt. The very fashionable classical names in Germany now are:

Girls	Boys
ANNA	BENJAMIN
HANNA	CLEMENS
JANA	FELIX
JOHANNA	JOHANNES
LENA	JONAS
LINA	LUCAS
LISA	VALENTIN

FRANCE

Short names are cool in France these days, according to our correspondents Rory Satran and Bruno Pradels, as are British names: style icon Jane Birkin's daughter Charlotte Gainsbourg has children named Alice and Ben, and Jane's other style-setting daughter is named Lou. Manon, from the hit movie *Manon of the Spring*, is still hot, as are the simple

Lea and Luca and some new Italian imports. But Amelie's star is finally dimming.

Girls

ALICE	FLAVIE	LUNA
ANAELLE	FLORA	MAELLE
ASSIA	ILONA	MAELYS/MAILYS
CHIARA	INÈS	MAEVA
CLÉA	LÉA	MANON
CLEMENCE	LÉONIE	NOLWENN
CYLIA	LILA	ROMANE
ELOÏSE	LILOU	SALOME
ELSA	LOLA	SELMA
FAUSTINE	LOU	

Boys

AMEDEO	LUCA	THEO
ANGELO	MAEL	THOMAS
ARTHUR	MALO	TOM
BEN	MATHIS	UGO
ELIOTT	MATTEO/MATHEO	
EMILIEN	MAXENCE	
ENZO	NATHAN	
ERWAN	NINO	
KILLIAN	NOLAN	
LÉO	OSCAR	
LÉON	SACHA	

Sahara

Place Names

As a category, place names have been so well visited over the past decade that many selections from this group are no longer distinctive enough to be considered truly cool. However, some individual place names retain a fresh feeling and so still merit the official Seal of Coolness. For the most part, these are the more unusual choices as well as the more exotic places – or KINDS of places, which include rivers and national parks. However, a few old favourites – India stands out – are as cool as they ever were. Some place names can be used for boys but most now veer toward the feminine side.

ABILENE

AFRICA

ALAMO

ALBANY

ANDORRA

ANTARCTICA

AQUITAINE

ARABIA

ARAGON

ASPEN

ASSISI

ATLANTA

ATLANTIS

AVALON

BERLIN

BIMINI

BOLIVIA

BOSTON

BRASILIA

BRAZIL

BRISTOL

CAIRO

CALAIS

CALEDONIA

CAMDEN

CARAGH

CASPIAN

CATALINA

CAYMAN

CEYLON

CHARLESTON

CLUNY

COLOMBIA

CONNEMARA

CORSICA

CUBA

CYPRUS

DELPHI

DENVER

DOVER

DUBLIN

DUNE

ELBA

ENGLAND

EVEREST

GALWAY

GLASGOW

HARLEM

HAVANA

HOLLAND

HUDSON

IBERIA

INDIA

INDRA/INDRE

IRELAND

JAMAICA

JERSEY

KENYA

KINGSTON

KYOTO

LOUISIANA

LOURDES

MEMPHIS

MIAMI

MILAN

MOROCCO

NAIROBI

NILE

ODESSA

OLYMPIA

PALERMO

PANAMA

PERSIA

PERU

PHILIPPINE

PORTLAND

QUEBEC

QUINTANA

RALEIGH

RIO

ROMA

ROMANY

SAHARA

SALEM

SAMARA

SAMOA

SENEGAL

SEVILLA

SICILY

SIENA

SONOMA

SONORA

TAHITI

TANGIER

TIBET

TRENTON

TRINIDAD

UMBRIA

VALENCIA

VENICE

VIENNA

YORK

ZION

Jezebel & Jane

Bad Girl/Good Girl Names

It may be difficult for people on the brink of parenthood to acknowledge this, but it's cool to be bad. It was cool when you were younger . . . and it's still going to be cool when your baby-to-be is a lot lot older. And in this age of extremes, it's also cool to be good. Prime example: Madonna, whose own name makes both lists, gave her daughter the saintly name of Lourdes, the place where it is believed that the Virgin Mary miraculously heals the sick, but calls her by the sultry nickname Lola. For further illustration of the bad girl/good girl concept and more name ideas for your own angelic hellion, consult the following list:

Bad Girls

APHRODITE

ASIA

BATHSHEBA

BILLIE

CAYENNE

CLEO

COCO

DELILAH

DESDEMONA

DIVA

DIXIE

DOMINIQUE

EGYPT

FANNY

FIFI

FLAME

GIGI

JEZEBEL

LANA

LILITH

LOLA

LULU

MABEL

MADONNA

MAISIE

MAMIE

MITZI

MONIQUE

PANDORA

PEACHES

PORTIA

QUEENIE

RAMONA

RAVEN

RIPLEY

ROXANNE

ROXIE/ROXY

RUBY

SADIE

SALOME

SCARLETT

SHEBA

STORM

TALLULAH   XENA
TEMPEST
TRIXIE   YASMINE

VENUS   ZULEIKA

Good Girls

ABIGAIL   FAITH
ALICE   FELICITY
ALICIA   FLEUR
ALLEGRA   FLORA
ANEMONE   FLOWER
ANGELICA   FRANCES
ANNA   FREESIA
ARIEL
                  GRACE
BAY
                  HELEN
CARA   HONOR
CHARITY   HOPE
CHASTITY
CLAIRE   JANE
COMFORT   JULIA
CONSTANCE   JUSTICE

                  LAKE
DULCY   LAURA

ELEANOR   LEAH
ESTHER   LILAC

LILIA	PRISCILLA
LOUISA	PRUDENCE
LOURDES	
	RACHEL
MADONNA	ROSE
MARGARET	RUTH
MARIA	
MARIAN	SERAPHINA
MARTHA	SERENA
MERCY	SILENCE
MIMOSA	SUNDAY
MODESTY	
	TEMPERANCE
NORA	TILLIE
	TRUE
PANSY	
PATIENCE	UNITY
PETUNIA	
	VERITY
POLLY	
	VIRGINIA
POSEY	
PRIMROSE	WILLOW

Alfie

Nickname Names

We've heard lots about Jack and Harry, but now other ordinary down-to-earth short forms of traditional English names – Joe not Joseph, Bobby instead of Robert – are newly cool. Even the once-embarrassing names of mouldering old relatives – Dick and Betty, for instance – are returning to the light.

Girls

BEA	COCO
BETTY	
	DAISY
CHARLIE	DIXIE

DOTTIE	MAISIE
	MAY
ELLIE	MILLIE
EDIE	MOLLY
EVIE	
	PATSY
FLO	PIPPA
HONEY	
	ROSIE
KITTY	
	TRIXIE
LIBBY	
LULU	WINNIE

COOLEST
COWBOY NAME
• • •
Autry

Boys

ALFIE	JAKE
ARCHIE	JIMMY
	JOE
BARNEY	
BERNIE	MAC/MACK
BILLY	
	NED
BOBBY	
	RAY
CHARLIE	RUDY
DICK	
	SAM
FRANK	STAN
FRED	
	TOBY
GUS	TOM

Macauley

Mac Names

We've heard in the past few years of a lot of Macken-zies, McKennas and McKaylas – in a wide array of spellings. Cute, maybe, but no longer are these three names cutting-edge cool. So, too, in recent years have other surname-names enjoyed widespread popularity, rendering such waspy favourites as Parker and Cooper beyond cool.

What's cool now is a combination of the two trends: surname-names with the Mac (think Macaulay, as in Culkin) prefix. Of course, the coolest surnames are the ones you can lay genuine claim to from your family tree. But here's one idea: you can honour an ancestor by putting the Mac prefix (which signifies 'son of') before his first name, so grandpa Arthur inspires baby Macarthur. Authentic or not, used for girls or boys, these choices are undeniably cool:

MACALLISTER	MCCARTHY
MACARDLE	MCCOY
MACARTHUR	MCDERMOTT
MACAULAY	MCELROY
MACKAY	MCENROE
MACLAREN	MCEWAN
MACLEAN	MCGRATH
MACMILLAN	MCKEON
MACREA	MCKINLEY
MAGEE	MCLAUGHLIN
MAGINNES	MCLEOD
MAGUIRE	MCMANUS
MCADAM	MCNALLY
MCAVOY	MCNEIL
MCCABE	MCPHERSON
MCCAREY	

Orlando

O Names

We said it in our very first baby-naming book, *Beyond Jennifer & Jason*, and we say it still: names that begin or end with the letter 'o' are cool. Thankfully, the 'o' names remain unsullied, appealing choices all, especially (though there are a few feminine selections in this group) for boys. The options, of course, range far beyond those offered here, especially considering the entire world of Latinate names. This group just gives you a start.

ALAMO	**ALONZO**
ALDO	**AMEDEO**

ANTONIO	DJANGO
APOLLO	DURANGO
ARLO	
ARMANDO	ECHO
ARNO	ELMO
	EMILIO
BENECIO/	ENZO
BENICIO	
BENNO	FERNANDO
BO	FRISCO
BRUNO	
	GIACOMO
CAIO	GIORGIO
CAIRO	
CALICO	HORATIO
CALYPSO	HUGO
CAMEO	
CARLO	INDIGO
CATO	INDIO
CICERO	INIGO
CLAUDIO	IVO
CLEO	
COLORADO	JERICHO
CONSUELO	JETHRO
COSMO	
	KYOTO
DANILO	
DIEGO	LAREDO
DINO	LEANDRO

LEO	ODILE
LEONARDO	ODIN
LIDO	ODION
LORENZO	OLAF
LUCIANO	OLGA
	OLIVER
MARCO	OLIVIA
MARINO	OLIVIER
MASSIMO	OLWEN
MILO	OLYMPIA
MONTEGO	OMAR
MOROCCO	OONA
	OPHELIA
NAVARRO	OREN
NEMO	ORIANA
NICO	ORILIO
NICOLO	ORION
NILO	ORLANDO
	ORLY
O'BRIEN	ORSINO
O'HARA	ORSON
O'KEEFE	OSCAR
OAK	OTIS
OBADIAH	OTTILIE
OBERON	OTTO
OCEAN	OWEN
OCTAVIO	OZ
ODESSA	OZIAS
ODETTE	

PABLO	SCORPIO
PAOLO	SERGIO
PEDRO	SHILOH
PHILO	STEFANO
PIERO	
PLACIDO	TADDEO
PLATO	THEO
PRIMO	
PROVO	VIGGO
	VITO
RENO	VITTORIO
REO	
RIO	WALDO
ROCCO	
RODRIGO	ZENO
ROLLO	

COOLEST

PALINDROME NAME

• • •

Otto

Tilly

Boho Chic Names

There is a certain kind of name that is considered cool by that segment of the upwardly mobile yet politically correct population one might think of as bohemian. Bohos like distinctive things but abhor ostentation; they have good taste but disdain convention; they appreciate the classics but prefer them with a modern twist. Most but not all of the names they favour are to the left of the most popular list, but far to the right of most choices in this book. You'll see boho chic names on the registers of smart nursery schools, hear them in the playgrounds of affluent neighbourhoods, and you may like them yourself. And why not? They're good names, classic as well as cool, embodying style along with history. The only problem is that you may hear them far more than you want to in the years to come.

Girls

ALEXA	EDIE
ALLEGRA	EDITH
ANABELLA	ELEANOR
ANNA	ELIZA
ANNABEL	ELSPETH
ANWEN	EUGENIE
ARABELLA	EVA
AUDREY	EVE
AVA	EVIE
BELLA	FAYE
BRIONY/BRYONY	FELICITY
	FIONA
CAMILLA	FLORA
CARA	FLORENCE
CARINA	FRANCES
CAROLINA	FREYA
CECILY	
CLAIRE	GABRIELLA
CLARA	GEMMA
CLAUDIA	GEORGIA
CLEMENTINE	GRACE
CLOVER	
CRESSIDA	HELENA
	HERMIONE
DAISY	HONOR
DAPHNE	HONORA
DOROTHEA	HOPE

IMOGEN
INDIA
IRIS
ISABELLA
IVY

JACQUELINE
JESSAMINE
JESSAMY
JOCASTA
JOSEPHINE
JUDE
JULIA
JULIANA
JULIET

KERENZA

LAURA
LEATRICE
LEILA
LETTICE
LIBBY
LILA
LILIAN
LILY
LOLA
LUCY

MABEL
MADELEINE
MAEVE
MARGARET

MATILDA
MAUDE
MAYA
MIA
MIRANDA
MYFANWY

NATALIE
NATALYA
NATASHA
NELL
NICOLA
NORA

OLIVIA
ORLA

PHOEBE
PIPER
PIPPA
POLLY
POPPY

RHIANNON
RHONWEN
ROSE
RUBY

SADIE
SASHA
SOPHIA
SORCHA
STELLA

SUSANNAH

TAMSIN
TESS
TILLY

UNA/OONA
UNITY

VIOLET
VIRGINIA

WILLA

ZOE

Boys

AIDAN

ALEX

AMBROSE

ANDREW

ANGUS

ARCHIE

AUGUSTINE

BALTHAZAR

BARNABY

BARNEY

BASIL

CALEB

CALLUM/CALUM

CALVIN

CHRISTIAN

CLAY

COLE

COLIN

CORMAC

CRISPIN

DASHIELL

DECLAN

DOMINIC

DUNCAN

EAMON

ELIJAH

EMMETT

ETHAN

EUAN/EWAN

EZRA

FELIX

FERGUS

FINLAY

FINN

FORREST

FRASER

GABRIEL

GREGORY

GUS

HAMISH

HARRISON

HARRY

HENRY

HOMER

HUGH

HUGO

INIGO

ISAAC

ISAIAH

JACKSON	OLIVER
JASPER	OSCAR
JOE	OWEN
JONAH	
JONAS	PATRICK
JUDE	PIERS
JULIAN	
	QUENTIN
	QUINN
KIAN	
KIERAN	RAYMOND
KILLIAN	REDMOND
	REECE/RHYS
LACHLAN	REED
LAIRD	REX
LEO	REYNOLD
LEWIS/LOUIS	ROHAN/ROWAN
LORCAN	ROLAND
LUCA	RONAN
LUCAS	RORY
	RUPERT
MALACHY	
MALCOLM	SEAMUS
MARCUS	SEBASTIAN
MILES	SPENCER
NATHAN	TOBIAS
NATHANIEL	TRISTAN
NED	VICTOR
NOAH	WALKER
NOEL	WYATT

· 43 ·

Q

Nicknames

Sometimes the whole nature of a name can be changed and 'cooled' by using a fresh-sounding nickname, either as a short form or on its own. Many of the names that are heard today – such as Molly, Kate, Jack and Toby – began as more informal versions of standard names. Here are some ideas for new-millennium nicknames, some of them revivals of old favourites, some of them foreign imports:

ASH	Asher, Ashley
BAS	Sebastian
BENNO	Benjamin
BETTA	Elizabeth
BIDU	Bridget
BRAM	Abraham
BREE	Briana
CALE	Caleb
CAM	Camilla
CARLO	Charles
CARO	Caroline
CASO	Cassandra
CAT	Catherine
CHAN	Chandler
CHARLIE	Charlotte
CHARTY	Charlotte
CHAY, CHAZ	Charles
CIA	Cynthia
CINDA	Cynthia, Lucinda
CLEM	Clementine
COZ	Cosmo
DAISY	Margaret
DASH	Dashiell
DEBO, DEBS	Deborah
DEX	Dexter
DEZ, DEZI	Desmond

DIX	Richard
DOE	Dorothea
DORO	Dorothea, Dorothy
DREA, DREE	Alexandria, Andrea
DREW	Andrew
DUNN	Duncan
FRANCE	Frances
FEE	Fiona
FLORY	Florence
FRITZI	Frederica
GEORGE	Georgia
GORE	Gordon
GRAM	Graham
GUS	Angus, August, Augusta
IBBY	Isabel
IMMY	Imogen
IZZY	Isaac, Isabel, Isadora
JAX	Jackson
JEM	Jemima, Jeremy
JULES	Julia, Julie
KAT	Katharine
LAURO	Laurence
LETTY	Elizabeth

COOLEST
ROYAL NAME
• • •

George

LIAM	William
LIV, LIVIA, LIVY	Olivia
LOLA	Dolores, Lolita, Lourdes, Paloma
LOLO	Caroline
LULU	Louise
MABBS	Mabel
MAGO	Margaret
MAISIE	Margaret
MAMIE	Mary
MANO	Emanuel
MASO	Thomas
MELIA	Amelia
MITZI	Mary, Miriam
MO	Maureen
NED	Edward
NELL, NELLY	Eleanor, Ellen, Helen
NESSA	Vanessa
NICO	Nicholas
O	Olivia, Otis, Owen
OZ, OZZIE	Oscar
PATIA	Patricia
PIP	Phillip
PIPPA	Philippa
POLLY	Mary, Pauline

POM	Thomas
PRU	Prudence
Q	Quentin, Quincy
RAFE	Ralph, Raphael
SACHA, SASHA	Alexander, Alexandra
SADIE	Sarah
SEB	Sebastian
SIMM, SIMS	Simeon, Simon
SKY	Schuyler, Skyler
SUKEY	Susannah
TADDEO	Theodore
TANSY	Anastasia
TESS, TESSA	Teresa
TIBBIE	Elizabeth
TONIO	Anthony
TRIXIE	Beatrix
TRU	Truman
VAN	Vanessa
WILLS	William
XAN, ZAN	Alexander
Z	Zachary et al.
ZANDER	Alexander

II. COOL COOL

. . .

Famous Names

Sienna

Celebrity Names

A cool name seems as essential an ingredient of stardom today as a well-sculpted body and a killer smile, a fact that can hardly be lost on parents in search of a name that will help launch their child in the world. Some of these names – Keira is a notable example – are inspiring thousands of namesakes, but their real power as a group is in making parents feel that, when it comes to names, special means beautiful, talented and famous. While names of current stars are most influential, some favourites from the past – Audrey and Ava, for instance – are also proving inspirational.

ADRIEN Brody

AIDAN Quinn

ANASTACIA

ANGELINA Jolie

ASHANTI

ASHTON Kutcher

AUDREY Tatou

AVRIL Lavigne

BALTHAZAR Getty

BECK

BENICIO Del Toro

BEYONCÉ Knowles

BJORK

BLU Cantrell

BONO

BRYCE DALLAS Howard

CALISTA Flockhart

CAMERON Diaz

CATE Blanchett

CHAKA Khan

CHARLIZE Theron

CHINA Chow

CILLIAN Murphy

CLE Du Vall

CORIN Redgrave

CRISPIN Glover

CUBA Gooding, Jr

DAMIAN Lewis

DARYL Hannah

DELROY Lindo

DEMI Moore

DENZEL Washington

DERMOT Mulroney

DIVA Zappa

DJIMON Hounsou

DIDO

DONOVAN Leitch

DOUGRAY Scott

DREW Barrymore

DULE Hill

EDIE Sedgwick

ELLE Macpherson

ELMORE Leonard

EMMA Thompson

EMO Phillips

ENRIQUE Iglesias

ENYA

EVA Longoria

EWAN McGregor

FAMKE Jannsen

FARRAH Fawcett

FELICITY Huffman

GABRIEL Aubry

GISELE Bündchen

GLENN Close

GWYNETH Paltrow

HALLE Berry

HARRISON Ford

HAYDEN Christenson

HEATH Ledger

HELENA Bonham Carter

HUGH Jackman

ILEANA Douglas

IOAN Gruffudd

IONE Skye

ISLA Fisher

JADA Pinkett-Smith

JADE Jagger

JAVIER Bardem

JEMIMA Khan

JENA Malone

JOAQUIN Phoenix

Angelina JOLIE

JOSS Stone

JUDE Law

JULIETTE Binoche

KACEY Ainsworth

KEANU Reeves

KEIRA Knightley

KIEFER Sutherland

KIKA Markham

KOO Stark

KYRA Sedgwick

LAKE Bell

LEELEE Sobieski

LEONARDO DiCaprio

LIAM Neeson

LIBERTY Ross

LIVE Schreiber

LIV Tyler

Jennifer LOVE Hewitt

LULU

MACY Gray

MAGENTA Devine

MARIAH Carey

MENA Suvari

MILLA Jovovich

MINNIE Driver

MISCHA Barton

MOBY

MOON Unit Zappa

NATALIE Portman

NEVE Campbell

OLIVIER Martinez

ORLANDO Bloom

OWEN Wilson

PARIS Hilton

PARKER Posey

PETULA Clark

PIERCE Brosnan

PINK

PORTIA de Rossi

REESE Witherspoon

RHYS Ifans

ROMOLA Garai

RONAN Keating

ROSAMUND Pike

ROSARIO Dawson

RUPERT Everett

SADE

SAFFRON Burrows

SALMA Hayek

SCARLETT Johansson

SHAKIRA

SHALOM Harlow

SIENNA Miller

SIGOURNEY Weaver

SKEET Ulrich

STELLA McCartney

STOCKARD Channing

SUMMER Phoenix

SURANNE Jones

TALISA Soto

TATUM O'Neal

TAYE Diggs

TEA Leoni

THANDIE Newton

THORA Birch

TIGER Woods

TILDA Swinton

TUPAC Shakur

TYRA Banks

TYSON Beckford

ULRIKA Jonsson

UMA Thurman

VENDELA

VENUS Williams

VIGGO Mortensen

VIN Diesel

VING Rhames

VIVICA Fox

WINONA Ryder

WYCLEF Jean

ZOOEY Deschanel

Petal

Movie Character Names

The only names cooler than stars' names right now are the names of the characters they play. In fact, with the exception of Jack, which seems to be the name of the male lead in every other movie these days, characters' names veer from the unusual to the outlandish. A few, such as Trinity from *The Matrix*, are moving up the popularity charts. Others may prove inspirational to you. Here is a

COOLEST

SOUTHERN BELLE NAME

...

Delilah

sampling of cool character names along with the stars who play them and the films in which they appear.

AKASHA	Aaliyah	*Queen of the Damned*
AMÉLIE	Audrey Tautou	*Amélie*
AMSTERDAM	Leonardo DiCaprio	*Gangs of New York*
ARWEN	Liv Tyler	*The Lord of the Rings*
AZRAEL	Jason Lee	*Dogma*
BARTLEBY	Ben Affleck	*Dogma*
	Christian Glover	*Bartleby*
BJERGEN	Drew Barrymore	*Wayne's World 2*
BONANZA	Rain Phoenix	*Even Cowgirls Get the Blues*
BULLSEYE	Colin Farrell	*Daredevil*
CASH	Don Cheadle	*The Family Man*
CASTOR	John Travolta/ Nicolas Cage	*Face/Off*
CHAKA	Chris Rock	*Jay & Silent Bob Strike Back*
CHASE	Nicole Kidman	*Batman Forever*
CHILI	John Travolta	*Get Shorty*
CHRISTABEL	Jennifer Ehle	*Possession*
CISCO	Mark Addy	*Down to Earth*
CLERICK	Christian Bale	*Equilibrium*
CLOVE	Jennifer Aniston	*The Thin Pink Line*
CLOVER	Angelina Jolie	*The Good Shepherd*
CODY	Elisabeth Shue	*Bad Girls*
COTTON	Liev Schreiber	*Scream 2*

CYRUS	Selma Blair	*Down to You*
DEMILLE	Robert Sean Leonard	*Driven*
DESI	Julia Stiles	*O*
DEVLIN	George Clooney	*Spy Kids*
DEX	Giovanni Ribisi	*The World of Tomorrow*
DOVA	Matt Dillon	*Albino Alligator*
DOYLE	Samuel L. Jackson	*Changing Lanes*
DOMINO	Keira Knightly	*Domino*
DRAVEN	Cuba Gooding, Jr	*In the Shadows*
ELEKTRA	Jennifer Garner	*Daredevil*
ELLE	Reese Witherspoon	*Legally Blonde*
ELMO	Samuel L. Jackson	*Formula 51*
EMBRY	Charlie Hunnam	*Abandon*
ETHNE	Kate Hudson	*Four Feathers*
EVANNA	Jessica Capshaw	*Minority Report*
FAUNIA	Nicole Kidman	*The Human Stain*
FRIDA	Salma Hayek	*Frida*
GREEN	Shalom Harlow	*How to Lose a Guy in Ten Days*
HANSEL	Owen Wilson	*Zoolander*
IMOGEN	Julia Stiles	*Down to You*
INES	Natalie Portman	*Goya's Ghosts*
JERZY	George Clooney	*Welcome to Collinwood*
JESMINDER	Parminder K. Nagra	*Bend It Like Beckham*
JJACKS *(sic)*	Keanu Reeves	*Feeling Minnesota*
JINX	Halle Berry	*Die Another Day*
JUBA	Djimon Hounsou	*Gladiator*

JUDE	Maggie Gyllenhaal	*Happy Endings*
KAENA	Kirsten Dunst	*Kaena: The Prophecy*
KORBEN	Bruce Willis	*The Fifth Element*
LEGOLAS	Orlando Bloom	*The Lord of the Rings*
LEHIFF	Colin Farrell	*Intermission*
LIDDA	Kirsten Dunst	*Luckytown Blues*
LOKI	Matt Damon	*Dogma*
LONGFELLOW	Adam Sandler	*Mr Deeds*
LUSSURIOSO	Eddie Izzard	*Revengers Tragedy*
LUX	Kirsten Dunst	*Virgin Suicides*
MACE	Samuel L. Jackson	*Star Wars: Episode II – Attack of the Clones*
MAXIMUS	Russell Crowe	*Gladiator*
MIRTHA	Penelope Cruz	*Blow*
MORPHEUS	Laurence Fishburne	*The Matrix*
NEO	Keanu Reeves	*The Matrix*
NOLA	Scarlett Johansson	*Match Point*
NOVALEE	Natalie Portman	*Where the Heart Is*
OBERON	Heath Ledger	*Paws*
ORORO	Halle Berry	*X-Men*
PADMÉ AMIDALA	Natalie Portman	*Star Wars: Episode II – Attack of the Clones*
PARIS	Marisa Tomei	*Dirk and Betty*
PELAGIA	Penelope Cruz	*Captain Corelli's Mandolin*
PETAL	Cate Blanchett	*The Shipping News*

PETUNIA	Fiona Shaw	*Harry Potter Series*
PISTACHIO	Dana Carvey	*The Master of Disguise*
PLUTO	Eddie Murphy	*Pluto Nash*
POLEXIA	Anna Paquin	*Almost Famous*
RHEYA	Natascha McElhone	*Solaris*
ROUX	Johnny Depp	*Chocolat*
SALA	Catherine Zeta Jones	*The Phantom*
SATINE	Nicole Kidman	*Moulin Rouge*
SCHMALLY	Rachael Leigh Cook	*Scorched*
SERENDIPITY	Salma Hayek	*Dogma*
SERLEENA	Lara Flynn Boyle	*Men in Black 2*
SHARONNA	Heather Graham	*The Guru*
SULLIVAN	Richard Gere	*Dr T and the Women*
TERRA	Rain Phoenix	*Facade*
TORRANCE	Kirsten Dunst	*Bring It On*
TOULA	Nia Vardalos	*My Big Fat Greek Wedding*
TRINITY	Carrie-Anne Moss	*The Matrix*
TRIP	Josh Hartnett	*The Virgin Suicides*
ULYSSES	George Clooney	*O Brother, Where Art Thou?*
VIVI	Ashley Judd	*Divine Secrets of the Ya-Ya Sisterhood*
WOO	Jada Pinkett Smith	*Woo*
WREN	Elijah Wood	*Black and White*
ZEE	Maggie Gyllenhaal	*Monster House*
ZINAIDA	Kirsten Dunst	*All Forgotten*

Klonoa

Video Game Names

Movie character names may seem both inspired and inspirational to parents in the first decade of the twenty-first century, but what of the next generation of parents-to-be, those raised not on movies and television but on video games? Their idea of a cool name is sure to be way wilder than that of parents today. These names from current popular video games will give you an idea of the kind of choices that might inspire the names of your grandchildren.

Girls	Boys
AOI	AIDYN
	AKUJI
KAIRI	ALUCARD
	ARC
LARA	ASH
MARIE	BANJO
PAI	CLOUD
	CRASH
QUISTIS	
	DANTE
RINOA	DAXTER
	DUKE
SAMUS	
SELPHIE	GOEMON
SHION	
	ICO
TAKI	
	JAK
YUNA	JOJO
ZELDA	KAGE

KAIN	RYU
KAZOOIE	
KLONOA	SPYRO
	SQUALL
LINK	
	TIDUS
MAJORA	TOAN
MAXIMO	
MUNCH	VYSE
PARAPPA	YOSHI
RAIDEN	ZELL
RYGAR	ZIDAN

Apple

Celebrity Baby Names

Baby-naming seems to have become a competitive sport on both sides of the Big Pond. The goal: to come up with the coolest name in town – a difficult task when your colleagues' babies are named Phinnaeus (Julia Roberts' twin), Apple (Gwyneth Paltrow and Chris Martin's daughter), and Rebel (along with Racer, Rocket, Rogue and Rhiannon the children of director Robert Rodriguez).

And what are we poor mortals to do, hearing such baby names? If not follow suit by naming our own children Apple and Rogue, then at least feel inspired to be a bit more adventurous in our choices of names. Just as celebrities influence our taste in clothes and hair and make-up, so too do they give us a new template for baby-naming.

Here are the coolest celebrity baby names of recent years, the famous parents who chose them, along with our thinking on why the names belong in this category.

ALASTAIR WALLACE *Penny Lancaster & Rod Stewart*
The enduring singer returned to his Scottish roots for the name of his seventh child, the middle name chosen in honour of his fiancée's grandfather.

AMELIA *Lisa Rinna & Harry Hamlin*
A long neglected Victorian name that's a cooler, more unusual choice than the similar-in-feel but more ordinary Amanda or Emily.

ANAÏS *Noel Gallagher*
The guiding force of Oasis undoubtedly took as his naming inspiration the famed novelist and diarist Anaïs Nin.

APPLE *Gwyneth Paltrow & Chris Martin*
This high-profile couple made international headlines when they chose this wholesome, rosy-cheeked fruit name for their daughter, setting off shock waves, but we can see it starting a trend – with Plums, Berrys, Cherrys, and even Lemons, Mangos and Papayas possibly populating schoolrooms of the future.

ASSISI *Jade Jagger*

Sir Mick's granddaughter was given this unique place name, evocative of the lovely Umbrian hill town, not to mention the benevolent St Francis. Her sister AMBA's name is an example of an altered spelling that works.

ATLANTA NOO *Amanda de Cadenet & John Taylor*

What's noo? Atlanta is one of the fresher sounding US place names, as are Avalon and Alabama.

AUDEN *Noah Wyle (daughter) / Amber Valletta (son)*

This softly poetic namesake of W.H. Auden has recently become a fashionable first name option, used for both sexes: definitely a cool name to watch.

AURELIUS *Elle Macpherson*

Given the supermodel seal of approval, this is one of the band of Roman Emperor names now in the realm of possibility.

AVA *Aidan Quinn / Heather Locklear & Richie Sambora / Reese Witherspoon & Ryan Philippe / John McEnroe / Hugh Jackman / Martina McBride*

One of the hottest current celebrity favourites and racing up all popularity lists, Ava radiates the sultry retro glamour of Ava Gardner.

BANJO PATRICK *Rachel Griffiths*

When the Oz-born actress chose this highly unusual name

for her son, many assumed it was a bizarre invention, but it has a legitimate tie to bush poet 'Banjo' Paterson. Banjo's younger sister has another tie to that continent, with the place name Adelaide.

BEATRICE MILLY   *Heather Mills & Paul McCartney*
The christening of Princess Beatrice brought this traditional name back into the public eye, and now it has further exposure as a Beatle baby. It has real family significance: Beatrice is the name of Heather's mother, and Milly was chosen to honour Sir Paul's aunt.

BECKETT   *Malcom MacDowall / Natalie Maines / Melissa Etheridge / Conan O'Brian*
An appealing surname-name rich in literary associations, both to the play and movie based on the life of Saint Thomas B. and to the Irish playwright-novelist Samuel B., it's recently become a red hot celeb favourite.

BELLA   *Eddie Murphy / Keenen Ivory Wayans / Mark Ruffalo*
Everything *ella* is stylish right now, and Bella, with its literally beautiful meaning, is one of the less overused, with a nice old world, grandmotherly veneer.

BETTY KITTEN   *Jane Goldman & Jonathan Ross*
Could any pair of names give off a more retro-camp vibe than this? – they sound like something lifted straight out of an American sitcom of the fifties. The couple's other off-spring, Honey Kinney and Harvey Kirby, have a similar feel.

BILLY RAY *Helena Bonham-Carter & Tim Burton*
This cool couple opted to put the freckle-faced nickname straight onto the birth certificate. A trend more and more parents are following, as in Alfie, Bertie, Freddie et al.

BLUEBELL MADONNA *Geri Halliwell*
Bluebell, though undeniably sweet and original, may be one of those names – much like those of fellow Spicebabies Brooklyn, Romeo, and Phoenix – that are reaching hard for cool and therefore don't achieve it.

BROOKLYN *Victoria Adams & David Beckham*
Named for the New York borough of his conception, the much-publicized first Beckham boy set off a veritable epidemic of ambi-gender Brooklyns. Brothers Romeo and Cruz could do the same.

CARYS *Catherine Zeta Jones & Michael Douglas*
Catherine Zeta Jones looked back to her Welsh roots when choosing this name, thereby giving it wider international recognition.

CASPAR *Claudia Schiffer*
German-born supermodel Schiffer took a similar path by selecting a name well used in her native country but considered pleasantly quirky in other parts of the western world. Let's hope her boy doesn't get too much Casper-the-friendly-ghost teasing.

COCO REILLY *Courtney Cox & David Arquette*
Though it has some fashion power via legendary designer

Chanel, Coco, like high-kicking friends Gigi and Fifi, has a lot of Gallic spirit but is short on substance.

COSIMA   *Nigella Lawson*
Elegant and exotic with classical music associations.

CRUZ   *Victoria Adams & David Beckham*
Once again, the Beckhams caused quite a stir when they chose this unisex Latino surname for their third son; it packs a lot of energy and charm into its single syllable.

DAISY BOO   *Jamie Oliver*
In the Top 50 names, Daisy is more hot than cool, but the playful middle name makes it stand out from the other daisies in the garden.

DASHIELL *Cate Blanchett/Lisa Rinna & Harry Hamlin/Alice Cooper*
A lot of dash and a touch of mystery thanks to detective writer Dashiell Hammett.

DEACON   *Reese Witherspoon & Ryan Philippe*
After giving their first child the trendy name Ava, this glitzy couple sought and found something unique for their second. It links up three current trends: occupational names, religious names and interesting names from one's family history – Charles Louis 'Deacon' Philippe was a distantly related early 19th century baseball player.

DELILAH   *Lisa Rinna & Harry Hamlin*
The quintessentially seductive name. How can a Delilah not be gorgeous, and cool?

DENIM KOLE   *Toni Braxton*
Named after Denham, a character in *To Sir With Love*. But substituting K's for C's is no longer kool.

DEXTER   *Diane Keaton*
A nerdy boy's name comes alive when given to a girl, and these days every name with an x in it is cool.

DIXIE DOT   *Anna Ryder Richardson*
This style maven has chosen names for her daughters – the other is Bibi Belle – that have tons of alliterative pizzazz.

EJA   *Shania Twain*
This unusual phonetic spelling of Asia gives the name a more masculine flavour.

ELIJAH BOB PATRICUS GUGGI Q   *Bono*
Don't try this at home.

ELLERY   *Laura Dern*
Ellery has gone from middle-aged, mid-century American mystery writer/detective to hot girl's name, a trend also happening with Elliot.

ESMÉ   *Tracy Pollan & Michael J. Fox/Samantha Morton/Anthony Edwards*
A captivating JD Salinger-inspired choice.

ESTHER ROSE   *Ewan McGregor*
A perfect companion name for sister **CLARA MATHILDE**,

Esther is a so–clunky–it's–fresh Old Testament name. A star's child has a head start on pulling off a name like this.

FINN   *Jane Leeves / Andrea Catherwood*

A name with enormous energy and charm, that of the greatest hero of Irish myth, Finn MacCool. Other related cool starbaby names: FLYNN (Elle Macpherson), FINNIGAN (Eric McCormack), FINLAY (Sadie Frost) and FINLEY (Chris O'Donnell), not to mention Julia Robert's phabulous Phinnaeus.

GAIA   *Emma Thompson*

Inspiration for this unusual name was found in classical mythology, Gaia being the primeval goddess of the earth.

GIGI CLEMENTINE   *Cynthia Rowley*

See Coco.

GOD'ISS LOVE   *Little Mo*

Some parents – especially those of the American Rapper persuasion – are moving beyond such religious/spiritual names as Genesis, Trinity, Miracle, Heaven and Nevaeh (Heaven spelled backwards) to more extreme examples like this and Praise Mary (DNX).

HARLOW   *Patricia Arquette*

Rather than go the first–name route to vintage Hollywood glamour, à la Ava and Audrey, this actress used the surname of the epitome of 1930s sex appeal, Jean Harlow.

HOMER   *Bill Murray/Richard Gere & Carey Lowell/Anne Heche*
Yes, Homer, one of the old-fangled names sidling back into favour, often used to honour an ancestor.

HONOR   *Tilda Swinton*
A renewed search for traditional moral values has prompted a revival of interest in 'virtue' names – Honor, Hope, Faith, Grace, Charity, Prudence, et al.

IRIS   *Sadie Frost & Jude Law*
Floral names like Rose and Lily are spreading like wildflowers, but these cool babynamers dared to pick a bloom that has been long out of fashion and so make it sound new again.

ISADORA   *Björk & Matthew Barney*
Lagging far behind cousin Isabella in popularity, perhaps due to too close a tie with tragic modern dancer Isadora Duncan or to fusty male version Isidore, Isadora is, we think, as did this quirky couple, worthy of revival.

JASPER   *Don Johnson*
An ideal choice that has both backbone and style, a combination difficult to find in a boy's name, with an artistic association with painter Jasper Johns.

JAYA   *Laura Dern & Ben Harper*
This exotic name of a Buddhist goddess makes an interesting alternative to the trendy Maya.

JAZ ELLE   *Steffi Graf & André Agassi*
The athletic energy of this championship couple is reflected
in their daughter's name. Jaz – often used as a nickname for
Jasmine and thus reflecting that trend – projects what can
only be called a jazzy image.

KAL-EL   *Nicholas Cage*
The birth name of Superman is unlikely to impart any
superhuman qualities to any mortal boy, and thus not as cool
as it thinks it is.

KEEN   *Mark Ruffulo*
Sharp.

KINGSTON   *Gwen Stefani & Gavin Rossdale*
This Jamaican place name and elegant British surname also
boasts the more regal yet user-friendly short form, King.

KYD MILLER   *Tea Leoni & David Duchovny*
Fortunately, this kyd is known by his middle name.

LAIRD   *Sharon Stone*
This celebrity mum chose to make her son the Laird of the
manor, with a name that has a pleasantly distinctive Scottish
burr.

LENNON   *Patsy Kensit & Liam Gallagher*
Naming a child after your cultural or other hero gives him
two cool advantages: a name with real meaning and a
positive image to reach towards. Rocker Zakk Wylde chose
Hendrix as his son's musical hero name.

LIBERTY   *Ryan Giggs*

A staunch, principled 'word' name chosen by this footballer.

LILLIAN AMANDA   *Baz Luhrmann & Catherine Martin*

Names usually take four generations to become cool again, and Lillian – last stylish a century ago – qualifies on that score, sounding fresher today than the more popular Lily.

LOLA   *Annie Lennox/Chris Rock/Denise Richards & Charlie Sheen/Carnie Wilson/Lucy Pargeter/Sara Cox*

Madonna's use of Lola as her daughter Lourdes' nickname brought Lola from the smoky back room to centre stage in terms of style. (Other lilting double-'l' names: LILA (Kate Moss) and LILY (Kate Beckinsale, Chris O'Donnell, Kathy Ireland and Johnny Depp).

LUCA   *Colin Firth*

The Italian roots of their mother are reflected in the names of the two Firth boys – Luca and Mateo – both of them easy to pronounce and assimilate.

MADDOX   *Angelina Jolie*

It's a surname-name with a twist, more offbeat than the upstanding Coopers and Walkers, and sexier too, thanks to the final '*x*'.

MAGNUS *Will Ferrell*

A powerful name with a magisterial quality, one of the newly unearthed ancient history artifacts — it dates back to Charlemagne, called Carolus Magnus, or Charles the Great.

MASON *Kelsey Grammar*

Fine for a boy, cooler for Frasier Crane's little girl

MATILDA *Michelle Williams & Heath Ledger*

So-far-out-it's-in possibility with Aussie connections, might be slated for a comeback after being chosen by this high-profile couple.

MATTEO BRAVERY *Benjamin Bratt*

Attractively energetic Latin version of the classic Matthew, combined with a new-fangled virtue word. Colin Firth is Dad to a Mateo.

MILLER *Stella McCartney*

An up-and-coming new occupational surname choice.

MILO *Ricki Lake / Liv Tyler / Camryn Manheim*

Jaunty.

MINGUS *Helena Christensen*

Not easy to pull off — recommended for dedicated jazz fans and supermodels only.

MOSES *Gwyneth Paltrow & Chris Martin*

Venerable, white-bearded Old Testament name brought into the 21st century as Apple's brother.

NAVY *Nivea & Terius Nash*
When R&B singer Nivea chose her daughter's name, she thought of it in terms of the colour and not the sea-going armed service.

OSCAR *Hugh Jackman*
This cheerful Victorian favourite is having a definite revival among stylish parents on both sides of the Atlantic.

PHOENIX CHI *Mel B*
Posh isn't the only Spice Girl with baby-naming talent. Phoenix is not only a trendy place name, but has mythological overtones symbolizing immortality.

PILOT INSPEKTOR *Jason Lee*
This film star took the trend of word/profession names and doubled it, adding a spelling variant for good measure.

PIPER *Gillian Anderson/Brian De Palma/Cuba Godding Jr.*
High energy and music.

POPPY HONEY *Jamie Oliver*
Poppy is cool, Honey a little gooey; when combined they sound more like recipe ingredients than a name.

PRESLEY *Cindy Crawford*
Not as in-your-face cool as Elvis but truer to the spirit of hip, Crawford is not the first to use this name: American country singer Tanya Tucker gave it to her daughter.

RACER, REBEL, ROCKET, ROGUE   *Robert Rodriguez*
This American film director (*Spy Kids, Once Upon a Time in Mexico*) is definitely of the school that believes in giving kids names they have to live up to – or live down.

RAFFERTY   *Sadie Frost & Jude Law*
One of the coolest of the Irish surnames, with a raffish quality all its own.

RIPLEY   *Thandie Newton*
A powerful, androgynous name, perhaps inspired by the commanding character played by Sigourney Weaver in the *Alien* movies.

ROAN   *Sharon Stone*
A strong, red-haired Irish name.

ROCCO   *Madonna*
The power of Madonna: making this muscle-bound he-man name cool outside of Sicily.

ROMEO   *Victoria Adams & David Beckham/Jon Bon Jovi*
Romeo, Romeo, where fore art thou? Thou art a previously quasi-taboo, overly dramatic Shakespearean exclusive that's now been legitimized as a baby name possibility by Posh and Becks, who chose it for their second son, a path followed by rocker Bon Jovi.

ROWAN   *Brooke Sheilds*
This friendly Irish surname was almost unheard of as a girl's

name before Brooke Shields made the gender switch; now it shows lots of potential as a likeable, unisex, Gaelic choice.

SACHA/SASHA *Kate Capshaw & Stephen Spielberg/Vanessa Williams/Jerry Seinfeld*
This Russian male nickname has really taken off for girls, given a boost by sensational Olympic skater, Sasha Cohen.

SAILOR *Christie Brinkley*
A name with personal meaning for Brinkley and her husband – always the foundation of a truly cool choice – that's inspired other occupation names like GARDENER and BAKER

SCARLET/SCARLETT *Sylvester Stallone*
Actress Scarlett Johannson has done more for this rosy name than Scarlett O'Hara ever did, making the name red hot.

SHEPHERD *Jerry Seinfeld*
Occupational surname with a pleasant, pastoral feel.

SHILOH NOUVEL *Angelina Jolie & Brad Pitt*
Despite rampant rumours that they were going to pick an African name, this high profile couple opted for a Biblical place name, meaning 'God's gift' or 'peaceful one' in Hebrew, for their daughter. Middle name Nouvel, French for 'new', is also the surname of one of Pitt's favourite architects.

STELLA *Melanie Griffith and Antonio Banderas/Elisabeth Shue/ Dave Matthews/Dan Ackroyd/Jennifer Grey/Peri Gilpin*
It seems all the names containing the letters 'ella' are magic

in celebrity land these days, which includes Ella itself, and the more Latinate extensions Stella, Bella, Isabella and Gabriella, all of which have an alluring, rhythmic sound.

STELLAN   *Jennifer Connelly & Paul Bethany*
An interesting Scandanavian import – both strong and somewhat exotic.

SURI   *Katie Holmes & Tom Cruise*
This obscure multi-cultural name hit the headlines as the daughter of TomKat, provoking heated debate among name experts as to its actual meaning.

TALLULAH   *Demi Moore & Bruce Willis / Simon LeBon*
The Willises launched the cool starbaby name concept when they chose SCOUT and RUMER as well as the more user-friendly Tallulah for their girls.

TRUE   *Forest Whitaker / Joley Fisher*
Inspirational, aspirational word name that works particularly well as a middle name. Joely Fisher named her daughter True Harlow: a real trend-blend.

VIOLET   *Jennifer Garner & Ben Affleck*
Soft and sweet but not shrinking, Victorian Violet, one of the prettiest of colour and flower names, chosen by these high-profile parents, has begun what is certain to be a rapid rise to popularity.

WALLIS   *Anthony Edwards*
Rescued from single-owner purgatory (via the Duchess of Windsor) and given new life.

WILLOW   *Will Smith & Jada Pinkett Smith*
A graceful nature application that also relates to Dad's name (as son Jaden's does to Mum's).

XAVIER   *Tilda Swinton*
This long neglected saint's name is being reassessed, what with the current enthusiasm for names with exes and zee sounds.

ZAHARA   *Angelina Jolie*
Delicate but strong multi-cultural name bestowed on her Ethiopian-born daughter by Angelina Jolie; Chris Rock used the abbreviated Zahra for his.

ZOLA   *Eddie Murphy*
As seductive as Lola, but with a distinctive, literary twist.

COOLEST
GLAMOUR GIRL NAME
• • •
Ava

Sahteene

Supermodel Baby Names

It's not enough that they're 19-year-old skinny, gorgeous, world-revered millionaires. They've got to have all that and babies, too – and not just ordinary babies, but babies with incredibly cool names. Here is the current crop of supermodel baby names:

AMAEL (boy)	Audrey Marnay
ARPAD FLYNN	Elle Macpherson
ARTHUR ELWOOD	Jasmine Guinness
AUDEN (boy)	Amber Valletta
AURELIUS CY	Elle Macpherson
CASPAR, CLEMENTINE	Claudia Schiffer
CECILY	Stella Tennant

DYLAN BLUE (girl)	Carolyn Murphy
ELLA	Lucie de la Falaise
ELLA RAE	Rhea Durham
FRANKIE-JEAN	Donna D'Errico
HAMZAH (boy)	Yasmin Warsame
HENRY	Heidi Klum
IRIS	Stella Tennant
JASMINE	Stella Tennant
KAIA JORDAN	Cindy Crawford
LENI	Heidi Klum
LILA GRACE	Kate Moss
LUCAS	Cecilia Chancellor / Natalia Vodianova
MARCEL	Stella Tennant
MINGUS LUCIEN	Helena Christensen
NIMA (boy)	Trish Goff
ORSON	Lucie de la Falaise
PRESLEY (boy)	Cindy Crawford
SAFFRON SAHARA	Yasmin leBon
SAHTEENE (girl)	Laetitia Costa
SYCLAR PIM (girl)	Frédérique van der Wal
SKYLA LILY LAKE	Liberty Ross
SCHUL	Liya Kebede
TALLULAH PINE	Yasmin leBon
TOBY COLE (girl)	Emme
WILLIAM DAKOTA	Angela Lindvall
YANNICK FAUSTO	Daniel Pestova

Monet

Artist Names

Artists (and architects and designers) are almost by def-inition cool, and their names are part of the package. Parents can capture some of that creative spirit by choosing one of these artist names for their baby, and at the same time give their child an inspirational role model. The following list encompasses both first (JASPER Johns) and last (CALDER) names, which have been drawn from all over the aesthetic map, from fine art to fashion.

AALTO	AMEDEO
ALAIA	ANSEL

AZZEDINE	EAMES
	EERO
BLAKE	ELLIS
BOHAN	
BRAQUE	FORD
	FRIDA
CALDER	
CARO	GABO
CELLINI	GAUGUIN
CHANEL	GEHRY
CHARDIN	GEORGIA
CHIRICO	GERRIT
CHRISTO	GOYA
CLAES	GRECO
COCO	
COLE	HARDY
CONRAN	HARTIGAN
CORNELL	HOMER
COROT	HOPPER
CRISTOBAL	
CURRIER	INDIANA
CY	INIGO
	ISSEY
DELAUNAY	IVES
DIX	
DONATELLO	JACKSON
DUFY	JASPER
	JUDD

KAHLO	MORISOT
KAMALI	
KENZO	O'KEEFFE
KLEE	
KRIZIA	PABLO
	PALOMA
LAUTREC	PEI
LÉGER	PELLI
LEONARDO	PIANO
	PICABIA
MAGRITTE	PICASSO
MAILLOL	PIET
MANET	PONTI
MANOLO	
MANZU	QUANT
MARIN	
MARISOL	RABANNE
MATTA	RAEBURN
MIES	RAPHAEL
MILLAIS	REM
MILLET	REMINGTON
MIRÓ	ROBBIA
MIUCCIA	RODIN
MONET	ROUSSEAU
MOORE	RYDER
MORANDI	
MOREAU	SARGENT
MORI	SERRA

SHAHN   VIEIRA
SIMONETTA   VIGEE
SOUTINE   VIONNET
SULLY

                 WESTON
TAMAYO   WILLEM
TITIAN   WINSLOW
TOULOUSE
TURNER   YVES

VALENTINA   ZANDRA
VALENTINO

Thelonious

Musician Names

Since musicians invented the concept of cool, where better to look for naming inspiration than to their own names?

AALIYAH	ARETHA
ABBA	ARLO
ADEMA	ARMSTRONG
AJA	ASHANTI
ALANIS	AUDRA
ALANNAH	AVRIL
AMADEUS	AXL

BASIA

BAEZ

BECHET

BECK

BENATAR

BESSIE

BEYONCÉ

BILLIE

BING

BIX

BJORK

BONO

BOWIE

BRAHMS

CAB

CALE

CALLAS

CALLOWAY

CARUSO

CHAKA

COLE

COLTRANE

CROSBY

DENVER

DEVO

DEXTER

DINAH

DION

DIXIE

DJANGO (pron. Jango)

DONOVAN

DUFF

DURAN

DYLAN

EARTHA

ELLA

ELLINGTON

ELTON

ELVIS

ENO

ENRIQUE

ENYA

ETTA

EVERLY

FABRIZIO

GARCIA

GARTH

GENESIS

GERSHWIN

GILLESPIE

GUTHRIE

HARRISON	MEHTA
HENDRIX	MILES
	MINGUS
IGGY	MORRISEY
ISAAC	MORRISON
	MOS
JABBO	MOZART
JACKSON	MULLIGAN
JAGGER	
JAHEIM	NASH
JOPLIN	NAT
	NELLY
KAI	NICA
KITT	
	ODETTA
LATIFAH	OTIS
LENNON	OZZY
LENNOX	
LIONEL	PIAF
LOUIS	PINK
LUCIANO	PRESLEY
MACY	QUINCY
MADONNA	
MAHALIA	RAMONE
MARIAH	RAVI
MARLEY	RAY
MCCARTNEY	RUFUS

SADE

SANTANA

SHANIA

SINEAD

SULLIVAN

TALIB

THELONIUS

VEGA

VERDI

VILLELLA (dance)

WOLFGANG

WYNTON

ZEVON

ZUBIN

Ludacris

Rap Names

Names of rappers take the galaxy of possibilities into a whole new universe, one that few parents, at least right now, will want to visit. Not to be too academic about this, but rap names have their basis in the double-naming tradition that dates back to the very beginnings of African-American culture, when slaves used the names imposed by their masters when white folk were around, and other names – African names, day names, nicknames – when they were with friends and family. So while it might be ludicrous at this point to think of naming your child after rapper Ludacris, the boundary-breaking nature of rap names

promises to inspire more adventurous choices – even if just
for their kids' nicknames – among hip-hop-loving parents in
the future. Here are a few of the rap names around today:

BIZZY	KANYE
BUSTA RHYMES	
	LIL BOW WOW,
CLIPS	LIL KIM,
	LIL ZANE
COMMON	
	LUDACRIS
DJ SHADOW	
DMX	MACE
DR DRE	MOS DEF
	MYSTIKAL
EAZY E1	
	QUEEN LATIFAH
50 CENT	
	RIHANNA
ICE CUBE	
ICE T	SISQO
	SNOOP DOGG
JA RULE	
JAY-Z	T-PAIN
J DILLA	TALIB KWELI

Dashiell

Literary Names

Literary inspiration can arise both from the names of authors and the characters they create. Here are some suggestions coming from the first and last names of writers ranging from Edgar Allen Poe to Zadie Smith, and characters from the pages of books spanning various periods of literary history. But in this category, as always, feel free to think about your own personal favourites.

AUTHORS

ALCOTT	CHANDLER
AMIS	CHEEVER
ANAÏS	CONRAD
ANGELOU	COOPER
APHRA	CRANE
AUDEN	
AUGUST	DANTE
AUSTEN	DASHIELL
AYN	DIDION
	DJUNA
BALDWIN	DYLAN
BALLARD	
BECKETT	ELIOT
BEHAN	ELLISON
BELLOW	EMERSON
BENET	EUDORA
BLAKE	
BLY	FITZGERALD
BRONTË	FLANNERY
BYATT	FORSTER
BYRON	FROST
CAIN	GALWAY
CARSON	GIDE
CARVER	GLASGOW

COOLEST
IRISH PLACE NAME
· · ·
Donegal

HADLEY	MALLARMÉ
HAMMETT	MAYA
HARPER	MCEWAN
HART	MEHTA
HARTE	MILAN
HEMINGWAY	MILLAY
HUGO	MORRISON
	MOSS
ISHMAEL	MUNRO
JARRELL	NERUDA
JERZY	NIN
JESSAMYN	NORRIS
JULES	
	O'CASEY
KEATS	
KEROUAC	PAZ
KESEY	PLATO
	PO
LAFCADIO	POE
LALITA	
LANGSTON	RALEIGH
LARDNER	RHYS
LE CARRÉ	RING
LONDON	ROALD
LOWELL	ROTH
	RUMER

SALINGER	TWAIN
SAROYAN	
SHAW	VIDAL

TENNESSEE	WALKER
TENNYSON	WILLA
THACKERAY	YEATS
THEROUX	
THISBE	ZADIE
THOREAU	ZANE
THURBER	ZOLA
TRUMAN	ZORA

CHARACTERS

FEMALE

ALABAMA	*Save Me the Waltz*	Zelda Fitzgerald
ALHAMBRA	*The Accidental*	Ali Smith
AMARYLLIS	*Back to Methuselah*	George Bernard Shaw
AMORET	*The Faerie Queen*	Edmund Spenser
ANTONIA	*My Antonía*	Willa Cather
ARABELLA	*The Pickwick Papers*	Charles Dickens
ARIADNE	*Heartbreak House*	George Bernard Shaw

AURORA	*Terms of Endearment*	Larry McMurtry
BATHSHEBA	*Far From the Madding Crowd*	Thomas Hardy
BRETT	*The Sun Also Rises*	Ernest Hemingway
BRIANA	*The Faerie Queen*	Edmund Spenser
BRIONY	*Atonement*	Ian McEwan
CANDIDA	*Candida*	George Bernard Shaw
CATALINA	*The High Road*	Edna O'Brien
CATRIONA	*Catriona*	Robert Louis Stevenson
CHARITY	*Martin Chuzzlewitt*	Charles Dickens
CHARMIAN	*Antony and Cleopatra*	William Shakespeare
CLARICE	*The Silence of the Lambs*	Thomas Harris
CLARISSA	*Mrs Dalloway*	Virginia Woolf
CLEA	*Alexandria Quartet*	Lawrence Durrell
CRESSIDA	*Troilus and Cressida*	William Shakespeare
CYANE	*Metamorphoses*	Ovid
DAHLIA	*Carry On, Jeeves*	P. G. Wodehouse
DAISY	*The Great Gatsby*	F. Scott Fitzgerald
DENVER	*Beloved*	Toni Morrison
DESDEMONA	*Othello*	William Shakespeare
DOMENICA	*Unconditional Surrender*	Evelyn Waugh
EMMA	*Emma*	Jane Austen
ESMÉ	*For Esmé – With Love and Squalor*	JD Salinger

EVANGELINE	*Evangeline*	Henry Wadsworth Longfellow
FAUNIA	*The Human Stain*	Philip Roth
FEATHER	*Bad Boy Brawly Brown*	Walter Mosley
FLEUR	*The Forsyte Saga*	John Galsworthy
GINEVRA	*Villette*	Charlotte Brontë
GUINEVERE	*Le Morte D'Arthur*	Sir Thomas Malory
HANA	*The English Patient*	Michael Ondaatje
HAYDÉE	*The Count of Monte Cristo*	Alexandre Dumas
HONORA	*Sea Glass*	Anita Shreve
HONORIA	*Bleak House*	Charles Dickens
	and *Babylon Revisited*	F. Scott Fitzgerald
HYACINTH	*The Princess Casamassima*	Henry James
ISADORA	*Fear of Flying*	Erica Jong
ISOLDE	*Tristan and Isolde*	
JACY	*The Last Picture Show*	Larry McMurtry
JADINE	*Tar Baby*	Toni Morrison
JULIET	*Romeo and Juliet*	William Shakespeare
JUNO	*Juno and the Paycock*	Sean O'Casey
KIKI	*On Beauty*	Zadie Smith
KINSEY	*A is for Alibi*, etc.	Sue Grafton
LOLITA	*Lolita*	Vladimir Nabokov
MAISIE	*What Maisie Knew*	Henry James
MALTA	*Bleak House*	Charles Dickens
MAMIE	*The Ambassadors*	Henry James

MARIGOLD	*Quartet in Autumn*	Barbara Pym
MARIN	*A Book of Common Prayer*	Joan Didion
MELANCTHA	*Three Lives*	Gertrude Stein
NARCISSA	*Sartoris*	William Faulkner
NENNA	*Offshore*	Penelope Fitzgerald
NERISSA	*The Merchant of Venice*	William Shakespeare
NINETTA	*Nicholas Nickleby*	Charles Dickens
NIOBE	*Metamorphoses*	Ovid
NOKOMIS	*Hiawatha*	Henry Wadsworth Longfellow
ORLEANNA	*The Poisonwood Bible*	Barbara Kingsolver
PANSY	*The Portrait of a Lady*	Henry James
PECOLA	*The Bluest Eye*	Toni Morrison
PEYTON	*Lie Down in Darkness*	William Styron
PILAR	*For Whom the Bell Tolls*	Ernest Hemingway
PLEASANT	*Our Mutual Friend*	Charles Dickens
PORTIA	*The Merchant of Venice*	William Shakespeare
PRAIRIE	*Vineland*	Thomas Pynchon
RAIN	*The Sandcastle*	Iris Murdoch
RIMA	*Green Mansions*	William H. Hudson
ROMOLA	*Romola*	George Eliot
ROSAMOND	*Middlemarch*	George Eliot
SABRA	*Cimarron*	Edna Ferber
SCARLETT	*Gone With the Wind*	Margaret Mitchell

SCOUT	*To Kill a Mockingbird*	Harper Lee
SETHE	*Beloved*	Toni Morrison
SHEBA	*Notes on a Scandal*	Zoe Heller
SIDDA/ SIDDALEE	*Divine Secrets of the Ya-Ya Sisterhood*	Rebecca Wells
STELLA	*A Streetcar Named Desire*	Tennessee Williams
SULA	*Sula*	Toni Morrison
TAMORA	*Titus Andronicus*	William Shakespeare
TAMSIN	*A Few Green Leaves*	Barbara Pym
TEMPLE	*Sanctuary*	William Faulkner
UNDINE	*The Custom of the Country*	Edith Wharton
VELVET	*National Velvet*	Enid Bagnold
VERENA	*The Bostonians*	Henry James
VIDA	*Vida*	Marge Piercy
VIVI	*Divine Secrets of the Ya-Ya Sisterhood*	Rebecca Wells
VIVIETTE	*Two on a Tower*	Thomas Hardy
ZORA	*On Beauty*	Zadie Smith
ZULEIKA	*Zuleika Dobson*	Max Beerbohm

MALE

AMORY	*This Side of Paradise*	F. Scott Fitzgerald
ARCHER	*The Age of Innocence*	Edith Wharton
ATTICUS	*To Kill a Mockingbird*	Harper Lee
AURIC	*Goldfinger*	Ian Fleming

AXEL	*Victory*	Joseph Conrad
BARLEY	*The Russia House*	John Le Carré
BARNABY	*Barnaby Rudge*	Charles Dickens
BEALE	*What Maisie Knew*	Henry James
BENVOLIO	*Romeo and Juliet*	William Shakespeare
BRICK	*Cat on a Hot Tin Roof*	Tennessee Williams
BROM	*The Legend of Sleepy Hollow*	Washington Irving
CASPAR	*Portrait of a Lady*	Henry James
CATO	*Henry and Cato*	Iris Murdoch
CHANCE	*Being There*	Jerzy Kosinski
CLEMENT	*Return of the Native*	Thomas Hardy
CLEON	*Pericles*	William Shakespeare
CODY	*Visions of Cody*	Jack Kerouac
CORIN	*As You Like It*	William Shakespeare
DARCY (surname)	*Pride and Prejudice*	Jane Austen
DARL	*As I Lay Dying*	William Faulkner
DORIAN	*The Picture of Dorian Gray*	Oscar Wilde
FENNO	*Three Junes*	Julia Glass
FITZWILLIAM	*Pride and Prejudice*	Jane Austen
GUITAR	*Song of Solomon*	Toni Morrison
GULLIVER	*Gulliver's Travels*	Jonathan Swift
HEATHCLIFF	*Wuthering Heights*	Emily Brontë
HIERONYMOUS	*City of Bones*	Michael Connelly
HOLDEN	*The Catcher in the Rye*	J D Salinger
ISHMAEL	*Moby Dick*	Herman Melville

JAPHY	*Dharma Bums*	Jack Kerouac
JARVIS	*A Tale of Two Cities*	Charles Dickens
JASPER	*The Pathfinder*	James Fenimore Cooper
JOLYON	*The Forsyte Saga*	John Galsworthy
JUDE	*Jude the Obscure*	Thomas Hardy
LAIRD	*In the Gloaming*	Alice Elliot Dark
LEMUEL	*Gulliver's Travels*	Jonathan Swift
LEVI	*On Beauty*	Zadie Smith
LOCH	*The Golden Apples*	Eudora Welty
MACON	*Song of Solomon* and *The Accidental Tourist*	Toni Morrison Anne Tyler
MAGNUS	*The Accidental*	Ali Smith
MARIUS	*Les Misérables*	Victor Hugo
MELCHIOR	*Brideshead Revisited*	Evelyn Waugh
MILO	*Catch-22*	Joseph Heller
MOR	*The Sandcastle*	Iris Murdoch
NEWLAND	*The Age of Innocence*	Edith Wharton
ORLANDO	*Orlando*	Virginia Woolf
PRAXIS	*Praxis*	Fay Weldon
QUEBEC	*Bleak House*	Charles Dickens
QUILLEN	*Sea Glass*	Anita Shreve
QUINTAS	*Titus Andronicus*	William Shakespeare
RHETT	*Gone With the Wind*	Margaret Mitchell
RILEY	*The Grass Harp*	Truman Capote
ROARK (surname)	*The Fountainhead*	Ayn Rand
RODION	*Crime and Punishment*	Fyodor Dostoevsky

ROMEO	*Romeo and Juliet*	William Shakespeare
RUFUS	*A Death in the Family*	James Agee
SANTIAGO	*The Old Man and the Sea*	Ernest Hemingway
SAWYER (surname)	*The Adventures of Tom Sawyer*	Mark Twain
SEBASTIAN	*Brideshead Revisited*	Evelyn Waugh
SENECA	*Babbitt*	Sinclair Lewis
SEPTIMUS	*The Mystery of Edwin Drood*	Charles Dickens
SHANE	*Shane*	Jack Warner Schaefer
SILAS	*Silas Marner*	George Eliot
TAFT	*End Zone*	Don DeLillo
TRISTAN	*Tristan and Isolde*	
TRISTRAM	*Tristram Shandy*	Laurence Sterne
UTAH	*Under Milkwood*	D. M. Thomas
VERNON	*Vernon God Little*	DBC Pierre
VIVALDO	*Another Country*	James Baldwin
WOLF	*The Sea Wolf*	Jack London
YANCEY	*Cimarron*	Edna Ferber
ZOOEY	*Franny and Zooey*	JD Salinger

And don't forget two of the coolest of all:

FABLE

STORY

Venus

Athlete Names

Most of the legendary stars of sports history, both in the British Commonwealth and the States, tend to have ordinary guy names like Joe and Jason and Martin and Mick, but the Christian names of some of the newer stars – as well as the surnames of the classics – offer options that go beyond the perimeters of that limited playing field:

AGASSI	ARJAN
ALCOTT	ARMSTRONG
ALI	ASHE
ALTHEA	AUSTIN

BANNISTER	GARFIELD
BECKER	GERAINT
BECKHAM	
BENOIT	HOGAN
BJORN	JORDAN
BORIS	JOSS
BRADMAN	
	KATARINA
CATT	KEWELL
COE	
COOPER	LAVER
CORBETT	LENNOX
CORRY	LLEYTON
CRESPO	
	MAGIC
	MALONE
DEMPSEY	MARBLE
DEXTER	MARTINA
DUBLIN	MCENROE
DUFF	MIA
	MOSS
EVANDER	MUTU
EVERT	
EVONNE	NEVILLE
EWING	
	PELE
FALDO	PICABO
FRAZIER	
	REDGRAVE
GILES	RIGBY
GABRIELLA	RIO

SARAZEN

SABO

SEBASTIAN

SERENA

SHAQUILLE

STIRLING

THIERRY

THORPE

TIGER

TUNNEY

TYSON

VENUS

VIJAY

WILKO

ZELMO

COOLEST
WINTERBABY NAME
• • •
Frost

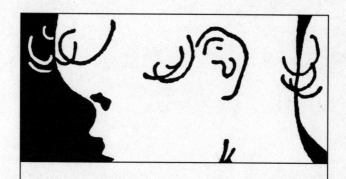

III. PRE-COOL
COOL

...

Old Names

Aurelia

Ancient Names

*O*ver the centuries, throughout the Western cultures, there have been thousands upon thousands of names lost to fashion. Okay, we can live without Baldric and Ethelbert, but many other ancient names – from Rome and Byzantium, from old England and Germany – deserve to be unearthed in the interest of cool. Here's a selection of worthy ancient names, from a range of eras and places, that have possibilities in the modern world.

Girls

ABELIA	DAMARIS
AMICA	DAMIANE
ANNIA	DECIMA
APHRA	DELICIA
APPHIAH	DENNOT
AQUILIA	DOMINICA
ARRECINA	DRUSILLA
ARRIA	
ATARAH	ELIZABELLA
ATHALIA	ELLOT
AURELIA	EPHRAM
AVITIA	
	FABIA
BASILIA	FANNIA
BEATA	FERELITH
	FLAVIA
CALVINA	
CAMPANA	
CANDIDA	GALLA
CESARIA	GAYNOR
CHAUNCEY	GWENORE
CLEMENCIA	
COLUMBA	HILARIA
CRISLI	HONORIA
CRISPINA	
CYRA	ISOLDE

JENNET

JOLECIA

JONET

JUNO

JUSTINA

LAURENCIA

LIVIA

MAHALA

MARABLE

MARCIANA

MELISENT

MERAUDE

MERIALL

MINERVA

MIREILLE (pron.

  Meer-ay)

MUCIA

NICASIA

OCTAVIA

PACCIA

PALATINA

PARNELL

PASSARA

PATERIA

PERPETUA

PERSIS

PETRONEL

PHILLIDA

PLACIDIA

PRIMULA

RAYNE

SABINA

SINETTA

TACE

TANAQUIL

TITIANA

TROTH

TULLIA

TURIA

VERINA

VISTILIA

VIVIANA

ZELINA

COOLEST
COUNTRY MUSIC NAME
• • •
Twain

Boys

AENEAS

ALBAN

ANDREAS

APOLLOS

ATTICUS

AUGUSTUS

AURELIUS

CASSIUS

CATO

CLAUDIUS

COSMAS

CYRUS

DEMETRIUS

LAZARUS

LOVELL

LYELL

MAGNUS

MARCELLUS

MAURUS

MAXIMUS

MENAS

NAZARES

PRIMUS

REMUS

ROMANUS

ROMULUS

SEPTIMUS

SEVERUS

STEPHANUS

TACITUS

TARQUIN

THEON

THURSTAN

TIBERIUS

TITUS

URBAN

ZEBEDEE

ZENO

Moses

Holy Names

Some of the coolest names we've come across in researching this book were found in the least likely of sources: the Bible and guides to the saints. If you want to know the provenance of the names that follow – who Lydia was in the Bible, for instance, or what made St Swithun so special – you're going to have to consult a source that deals with that sort of hard information. We're just here to tell you that these names are cool . . . and won't make the priest blanch at the baptismal font.

Girls

ADAH	KETURAH
ANASTASIA	KEZIAH
ANNICE	
APOLLONIA	LILITH
AQUILINA	LUCY
AZUBAH	LYDIA
	MARA
BARBARA	MICHAL
BERNADETTE	MORGANA
BETHIA	MORIAH
BIBIANA	
	NATALIE
CEARA	
CECILY	PRISCILLA
DARIA	RIONA
DEBORAH	RUTH
DELILAH	
DELPHINA	SANCHIA
DINAH	SAPPHIRA
	SARAI
EVE	
	TABITHA
FABIOLA	TALITHA
FAITH	TAMAR
	TATIANA
HADASSAH	THEA
JAEL	
JEMIMA	ZILLAH
JERUSHA	

Boys

ABEL

ABNER

ABRAHAM

ADLAI

ALBAN

AMBROSE

ANSELM

AUBREY

BARZILLAI

BASIL

BECAN

BENET

BENNO

BLASE

BOAZ

BROGAN

BRUNO

CALEB

CASSIAN

CLEMENT

CLETE

CONALL

CONAN

CRISPIN

CYPRIAN

CYRIAC

DECLAN

DONATE

DUNSTAN

EPHRAIM

ERASMUS

ESAU

EZEKIEL

EZRA

FABIAN

FELIX

FINNIAN

GABRIEL

GERMAIN

GERVASE

GIDEON

GILES

ISAAC

ISAIAH

JABEZ

JADON

JAPHETH

JAVAN

COOLEST
SPICE NAME
• • •
Saffron

JETHRO	RAPHAEL
JOAB	REMI
JOACHIM	REUBEN
JUBAL	ROMAN
JUDAH	RUPERT
JULIAN	
	SAMSON
KENELM	SAUL
KILIAN	SEBASTIAN
	SIMEON
LAMBERT	SIMON
LAZARUS	SIXTUS
LEMUEL	SWITHUN
LEVI	
LINUS	
LUCIAN	TIARNAN
	TITUS
MALACHI	TOBIAH
MATTHIAS	
MICAH	URBAN
MOSES	
	VITAL
NOË	
	WOLFRAN
OMAR	WOLSTON
OSWIN	
PIRAN	ZACHARIAS
	ZEBEDIAH
QUENTIN	ZEDEKIAH

BIBLICAL PLACE NAMES

ABILENE	JERICHO
ADAMAH	
AZEKAN	KEILAH
BETHANY	PELLA
BOZRAH	PETRI
CALAH	SAMARIA
CARMEL	SELA
	SHEBA
EDEN	SHILOH
GAZA	TAMAR
IVAH	ZION

Edmund

British Royal Names

When the newest British royal baby was born a month early, the world held its breath praying for her health…and anticipating her name. The playful Daisy was suggested as a possibility, but the final choice, Louise, was a royal standard. Cool? Marginally, in a stodgy kind of way. Beatrix and Eugenie were hands-down cooler choices, and so was Zara in its day.

Still, combing the royal rosters of England and Scotland, from the Saxons to the present day, produces many interesting options. This list includes not only the names of ancient kings and queens, but those of present-day little lords and ladies.

Girls

ADELA

ADELIZA

AFRIKA

AGATHA

AGNES

ALBERTA

ALESIA

AMABEL

AMICE

ARABELLA

AUGUSTA

AVELINE

BENEDIKTE

BETHOC

BLANCHE

CECILY

CLAUDINE

CONSTANCE

CORDELIA

DONADA

DOROTHEA

EDITH

ELIZA

ELOISE

EUGENIE

EUPHEMIA

EUSTACIA

FEODORE

FRANCES

IDA

JACQUETTA

MATILDA

MAUD

MAY

MURIEL

OLGA

SAVANNAH

SIBYLLA

URSULA

Boys

ALBERT

ALFRED

ARCHIBALD

CONSTANTINE

DOFIN

DUFF

DUNGAL

EDGAR

EDMUND

FINLAY

GODWIN

HAMELIN

HAROLD

HUMPHREY

IVOR

LIONEL

LUDOVIC

MALISE

MILO

OCTAVIUS

OTTO

PTOLOMY

ROWAN

THEOBALD

WARWICK

Olimpia

Euroroyal Names

Sure, the non-British royals still name their children such old stalwarts as Louis and Alexandra. But they also make much more adventurous choices, from Zita to Achille. Here, culled from European royal birth announcements of the past few years, are some notable examples.

Girls

ALINA	ANASTASIA
AMICIE	ANTOINETTE
AMINA	ASSIA

DARIA	OLIMPIA
FAUSTINA	PAULINE
HELOISE	SANCIE
JANUARIA	VALESKA
	VANINA
LAETITIA	
LEONIE	ZITA
LEOPOLDINE	

Boys

ACHILLE	LEOPOLD
ALFONSE	LUDOVIC
CASIMIRO	MASSIMO
CONSTANTIN	
	NICODEMUS
GABRIEL	RODOLPHE
GRATIAN	
	TASSILO
IGOR	THAÏS
JULIUS	WANDRILLE
LENNART	

Murray

Grandpa / Granddaughter Names

Blame it on Sidney. This name with thick glasses, a snowfall of dandruff on its shoulders, and polyester trousers pulled up to its sternum sounds nothing less than charming, nothing less than cool when applied to a little girl. And so too can the other Old Man names here. Caution: **Do not attempt to bestow any of these names on a boy.** The world is not yet ready for another generation of male Seymours and Stanleys.

ALLEN   BARRY
ARTHUR

CECIL	PERRY
CYRIL	
	RANDOLPH
GARY	ROY
HOWARD	SEYMOUR
	SHELDON
IRA	SHERMAN
JAY	SIDNEY
	STANLEY
LAWRENCE	STUART
LYLE	
	THEODORE
MARSHALL	
MAURY	VAUGHN
MORLEY	VERNON
MURRAY	VINCENT
NEIL	WALLACE
NORRIS	WAYNE

COOLEST

VICTORIAN NAME

• • •

Jasper

Agnes

Old Lady Cool

If you like that fusty old feel but you're not ready to go all the way to Murray for your daughter, you might want to consider the elderly lady names here, cool by virtue of their very disdain for fashion.

ADA	AUGUSTA
ADELIA	
AGATHA	BEATRICE
AGNES	BLANCHE
ANASTASIA	CLARA
ANTONIA	CLAUDIA

CORA	LAVINIA
CORDELIA	LEONORA
CORNELIA	LETITIA
	LOUISE
DORA	
DOROTHEA	MABEL
	MATILDA
EDITH	MAY
ELLA	MURIEL
ESTHER	MYRTLE
EUGENIA	
	OLIVE
FAY	
FLORA	PEARL
FLORENCE	
FRANCES	ROSALIND
	RUTH
HARRIET	
HAZEL	SYLVIA
HENRIETTA	
	THEODORA
IVY	
	VIOLA
JOSEPHINE	VIOLET
JUNE	
	WINIFRED
KAY	

Norbert

Names No One May Be Cool Enough For

You have to be pretty damn cool to name your kid Norbert, cool in that 'I like it and I don't care what the world thinks' kind of way. Except you're not the one who's going to have to deal with having the name Norbert when you play in the school football team. You're not the one who's going to have to introduce yourself as Norbert to girls in bars. In fact, if you think it's so cool, maybe you should change your own name to Norbert and not saddle a poor little kid with it.

The point: while we can appreciate the cool inherent in these clunky names, we fear that few human beings are cool enough actually to have one of them.

Girls

BERTHA	HEPZIBAH
BEULAH	HESTER
	HILDEGARDE
DORIS	HORTENSE
EDNA	
ELSIE	IRMA
ETHEL	JOYCE
EUNICE	
	MILDRED
FRIEDA	MYRNA
GAY	
GERTRUDE	PHYLLIS
GRISELDA	SHIRLEY
HELGA	WANDA

Boys

ARNOLD	EUGENE
BERNARD	FRANKLIN
BERTRAM	
BURTON	HARVEY
	HERMAN
DELBERT	HUBERT
	HYMAN
EDGAR	
ELMER	IRVING

JULIUS   SEYMOUR

                SHELDON
MAURICE
                SHERMAN
MELVIN
                SIEGFRIED
MERVYN

MILTON   VERNON

NORBERT   WILBUR

                WILFRED
OSBERT

OSWALD

IV. NEW COOL

...

Creative Names

Zaiden

Invented Names

For many prospective parents, the definition of a cool name is one that is unique. People are looking for names that will make their children stand out and apart from the crowd, and seek to achieve this either through creating a new spelling for an established name, or inventing a completely new name.

This taste for one-of-a-kind names is not surprising when you consider that many new mums and dads grew up with megapopular names themselves and felt that this robbed them of some of their individuality. In the 1970s and 1980s in the United Kingdom, for instance, there were legions of babies named Claire and Sarah and Emma, Andrew and David. This herd mentality on names was even more pronounced in the US, where for the entire 15-year period from 1970 to 1985 Jennifer was the number one name for girls. Jennifer became such a generic name that there are now Jennifer support groups on the internet and a Society for the Prevention of Parents Naming Their Children Jennifer.

In a larger sense, there is a general feeling of depersonalization and lack of distinctive identity in this era of ID codes and pin numbers, causing many parents to want to create a singular appellation for their children. And then there's the movement over the past decade or so toward increasingly unusual names, with new ethnic names, place names, surname-names, and words-as-names jumping into the mix. The parent who wants a truly distinctive name for her baby has to move further than ever away from the established roster of names.

For parents who want to create a unique name, here are some techniques:

1. Take a name whose sound appeals to you – this seems to work better for boys' names – change the first initial and play with the spelling if you like to make it rhyme. (We've also seen this trend happen with conventional names, with a somewhat more unusual choice – Mason – replacing its near-identical twin, Jason.)

AIDAN=BRAIDEN/BRAYDEN, CAIDEN/KADEN, JADEN/JAYDON,
    TAIDEN, ZAIDEN
ALLAN=CALLAN/KALLAN, DALLIN
AMOS=RAMOS, TAMOS
ANTON=CANTON, DANTON, JANTON, ZANTON
ARLO=DARLO, VARLO, ZARLO
BAILEY=ZAILEY
BARNEY=CARNEY/KARNEY, VARNEY, ZARNEY
CHRISTIAN=TRISTIAN
COLTON=BOLTON, DOLTON
DALTON=BALTON, CALTON, GALTON, RALTON
DARREN=JARREN/JARON, GARON, ZARREN
DERRICK=TERRICK, JERRICK, ZERRICK
DEVIN/KEVIN=BREVIN, JEVIN, TEVIN/TEVON
DYLAN=KYLAN, RYLAN
ETHAN=KETHAN, LETHAN
GABE=CABE, LABE, TABE, ZABE
GAVIN=DAVIN, KAVIN, TRAVON
HAYDEN=BRADEN/BRAYDEN, CADEN/CAYDEN/KADEN/
    KAYDEN, GRADEN, JAYDEN, SHADEN, TADEN, ZADEN/
    ZAYDEN
JACKSON=BRAXON, DAXON, MAXON, PAXON
JASON=BRASON, CASON, TAYSON
KEVIN=NEVAN, TEVIN
KIERNAN=TIERNAN
LEO=KEO, REO, TEO, ZEO
LOGAN=BROGAN, ROGAN
PIERCE=KIERCE

RILEY=BRILEY
TYLER=KYLER, SYLER, ZYLER
TYSON=BRYSON, DYSON, KYSON
WADE=CADE, DADE, ZADE
ZANE=THANE

2. Or you can approach it from the other direction and add another letter/syllable at the end:

ASH=ASHTON
BLAKE=BLAKEN
BRENT=BRENTON
BRYCE=BRYSON/BRYCEN
CADE=CADEN/CAYDEN/KADEN/KADIN/KAIDEN
CASE=CASON
CHASE=CHASEN
GREY=GREYSON, GREYER
JAY=JAYDEN, JAYLAN
KEITH=KEITHEN
KIRK=KIRKER
KYLE=KYLER/KYLAN
TRENT=TRENTON
TREY=TREYNOR, TREYTON

3. Another technique, this one as old as ElizaBETH and EuGENE, is to drop the first syllable or syllables, or even an initial letter of a name. These days, for instance, Drew and

Ward are cooler than Andy or Ed. Here are some other possibilities, but as with most recipes, feel free to improvise:

(H)	ARLEY
(Pris)	CILLA
(Mal)	COLM
(An)	DREA
(An)	JELICA
(Eze)	KIEL
(O)	LIVIA
(A)	LONZO
(A)	MANDA
(A)	MELIA
(Ca)	MILLA
(Ara)	MINTA
(Cor)	NELIA
(Va)	NESSA
(Vero)	NICA
(Law)	RENCE
(Ad)	RIAN
(Je)	REMY
(Gab)	RIELLA
(Ana)	STASIA
(Mon)	TANA
(Oc)	TAVIA
(Ma)	TILDA
(Syl)	VIA
(Ir)	VING

COOLEST
FLOWER NAME
• • •
Violet

(Ale) XANDER

(Ale) XANDRA

(A) ZIZA

NAME.DOT.COM

Accents and hyphens have been around for a long time, used mainly to indicate pronunciation or link a double name: think Renée-Thérèse. Then accents and hyphens started straying to places they didn't technically belong, all in the service of making names more interesting, more unusual, cooler. (Singer/actress Brandy called her daughter Sy'rai.) Now the new way to add punctuation interest to a name is with the — what else? — dot, as in the ubiquitous dot.com. Singer India.arie is perhaps the best-known example of this, but hip-hoppers Will.i.am and apl.d.apl of the Black Eyed Peas have joined in, transforming the practice from a one-person aberration to a trend.

Vrai

Foreign-word Names

Two of the coolest trends right now are word names and foreign names, so why not combine the two? We combed our own *diccionarios* for French, Italian and Spanish words that could make perfectly appropriate, attractive names for your baby, but no reason to stop here. Consider words from the language of your own ethnic background, be it Czech or Chinese, and add them to the list of your personal possibilities.

FRENCH

AÉRIEN	airy
ALÉA	chance
ALIZÉ	soft cloud
ALOUETTE	lark
AMANDE	almond
AMBRETTE	almond seed
AMÉRIQUE	America
ANGE	angel
ANNEAU	ring, ringlet
ATLANTIQUE	Atlantic
BECHETTE	little spade
BICHETTE	little doe
BIJOU	jewel
BLEU	blue
BONTÉ	goodness, bounty
BRIN	sprig
CADEAU	gift
CANDIDE	open, frank
CHATON	kitten
DÉJÀ	already
DELÀ	beyond
DÉLICE	delight

DIMANCHE	Sunday
DORÉ	gilded
ELLE	she
FABRIQUE	fabric
FLAMBEAU	flame, candle
FLEUR	flower
FLEURETTE	little flower
FRAISE	strawberry
GALETTE	flat cake
ICI	here
JADIS	in olden times
JAMAIS	never
JANVIER	January
JETON	marker, token
JOLIE	pretty
JUMELLE	twin
LARIGOT	ancient flute
LEXIQUE	lexicon, vocabulary
LIVRET	little book
LORIOT	oriole
LUMIÈRE	light
LUNE	moon

MAI	May
MAISON	house
MARDI	Tuesday
MARÉE	tide
MARGAY	tiger cat
MARRON	chestnut
MÉLILOT	sweet clover
MERISE	wild cherry
MIRABELLE	yellow plum
MOINEAU	sparrow
MUSIQUE	music
NEIGE	snow
NÉVÉ	compacted snow
NICHÉE	nest of young birds
PARC	park
PÊCHE	peach
PLAIRE	to please
POMME	apple
PREUX	gallant
REINE	queen
RIVAGE	shore
ROCHE	rock
ROUX	reddish brown
RUBAN	ribbon

SABINE	juniper tree
SAFRAN	saffron
SAISON	season
SAMEDI	Saturday
SANSONNET	starling
SATINÉ	satiny
SAVARIN	round cake
SÉJOUR	sojourn
SEMAINE	week
SOLEIL	sun
SOMMET	summit
SONGE	dream
TERRE	earth
TULIPE	tulip
VELOUTÉ	velvety
VICTOIRE	victory
VRAI	true
VRILLE	tendril
ZINGARO	gypsy

ITALIAN

ADAGIO	slowly, gently
AIO	tutor, teacher

ALBA	dawn
ALEA	chance, risk
ALITO	breath, light breeze
ALLEGRO	cheerful, merry
ALMA	soul
ALZATA	rising up, elevation
ANNATA	year's time
AQUILA	eagle
ARDESIA	slate
ARIA	air
AURETTA	gentle breeze
AURORA	dawn
BACCA	berry
BAIA	bay
BALIA	power, authority, also children's nurse
BALZO	leap
BELLEZZA	beauty
BENNATO	wellborn, generous
BIANCO	white
BLU	blue
BRIO	spirit, animation
CADENZA	cadence
CALA	cove, bay
CALIA	gold dust
CALLAIA	passage
CANNA	cane, reed

CAREZZA	caress
CIELO	sky
COLOMBA	dove
CORO	chorus
DANZA	dance, ball
DELFINO	dolphin
DESINATA	feast
DONNINA	good woman, clever girl
DOVIZIA	wealth, abundance
DUNA	dune
ELÈTTA	choice, elite
ÈLLERA	ivy
ELLISE	ellipse
FABBRO	inventor
FARO	lighthouse
FÈ	faith
FIAMMA	flame
FIERO	proud
FIORE	flower
FRANGIA	fringe
GÈLSO	mulberry
GEMELLA	twin sister
GÈMMA	jewel
GIADA	jade

GIOVANETTA	young girl
GRAZIA	grace
LAURO	laurel tree
LAVANDA	lavender
LILLA	lilac
LILLIALE	lilylike, white as a lily
LINDEZZA	neatness
LUNA	moon
MAGGIO	May
MANO	hand
MARÈNA	Morello cherry
MARRONE	maroon, chestnut
MASSIMO	maximum, supreme
MATITA	pencil
MATTOLINA	woodlark
MIRA	aim
MIRANDO	wonderful
MORGANA	mirage
NERO	black
NEVATA	snowfall
NEVE	snow
OLANDA	Holland
OMBRA	shadow

ONDA	wave
ORA	hour
PASQUA	Easter
PATRIA	native land
PÈRLA	pearl
PRIMA	first
RIVA	seashore
RIVO	stream, brook
ROANO	roan horse
SABBIA	sand
SALITA	ascent
SCALA	stairs
SERENELLA	lilac
STELLINA	little star
TAMIA	small squirrel
TERRA	earth
TRINA	lace
VALENTIA	skill, cleverness, bravery
VALLETTA	little valley
VENTURA	destiny, fate
VERO	true
VIA	way, street

VIOLETTA	violet
VITA	life
ZANA	basket, cradle

SPANISH

ALA	wing
ALBA	dawn
ALEGRIA	gaiety
ALETA	wing
ALONDRA	lark
ALZA	rise
AMAPOLA	poppy
ARO	ring, hoop
AURORA	dawn
AVELLANA	hazel tree
BAHIA	bay
BAYA	berry
BLANCA	white
BRIO	energy
CADENA	chain
CALA	cove
CANELA	cinnamon
CARICIA	caress

CEDRO	cedar
CHARRA	horsewoman
CIELO	sky
COLINA	hill
CONCHA	shell
CORTESIA	courtesy
CRUZ	cross
DIA	day
ESTRELLA	star
FLOR	flower
GALÁN	romantic hero
GALAXIA	galaxy
GANA	wish, desire
GARBO	poise
GAVIOTA	seagull
INDIO	Indian
ISLA	island
JABÓN	soap
JACA	pony
JACINTO	hyacinth
JAZMIN	jasmine
JOYA	jewel
JUBILO	joy

LAGO	lake
LEAL	loyal
LIENZO	linen
LOA	praise
LONA	canvas
LUNA	moon
LUZ	light
MAJO	nice
MAÑA	skill
MAREA	tide
MATIZ	shade, nuance
MEJILLA	cheek
MIRA	sight
OLA	wave
ORILLA	shore
PALOMA	pigeon, dove
PERLA	pearl
QUINTA	villa
REINA	queen
RENO	reindeer
RUBI	ruby

SABIO	wise
SEMILLA	seed
TALLA	carving
TIA	aunt
TIERRA	country
TIZA	chalk
TRAZA	appearance
VAJILLA	dishes
VALETA	weather vane
VEGA	fertile plain
VELADA	evening
VENTURA	happiness, luck
VIDA	life
ZAFIRO	sapphire

Pax

Spiritual Names

The post–September 11 world is more attuned to spirituality than ever. These names that suggest qualities we'd all like our children to aspire to fit our new definition of cool. While they seem as if they can work for both genders, most have been veering toward the feminine side. A few, such as Trinity, Destiny, Sky and Genesis, had already been moving up the girls' popularity lists; many of the others might be fresh suggestions for either a boy or a girl, or for a middle name if too extreme for a first.

ANGEL	INFINITY
ANSWER	
ARCADIA	JUSTICE
BLISS	KISMET
CALM	LIGHT
CHANCE	
	MIRACLE
DESTINY	MYSTERY
DIVINITY	
DREAM	PAX
	PEACE
EDEN	PROMISE
ETHEREAL	
EVER	REMEMBER
EXPERIENCE	
	SECRET
FORTUNE	SERENDIPITY
	SERENITY
GENESIS	SKY
GUARDIAN	SPIRIT
GUIDE	
	TAROT
HALCYON	TRINITY
HARMONY	TRUE
HEAVEN	TRUST

Indigo

Colour Names

Amber started it, and then Rose drove the point home. Now colour names have exploded beyond these once-cool favourites to include hues from the obvious – Gray and Teal – to the most exotic, from Azure to Zinc. Recently Blue has taken off, primarily as a middle name: Cher was one of the first to use it for her son Elijah, and now we have Jackson Blue (Maria Bello), John Travolta and Kelly Preston's gallicized Ella Bleu, and the rocker Dave (U2) Evan's daughter Blue Angel. A new entry was seen when superstar couple Uma Thurman and Ethan Hawke chose Roan Green for their son. The full spectrum:

ALIZARIN

AMETHYST

ANILINE

AQUA

ASH

AUBURN

AZURE

BEIGE

BRICK

BROWN

BUFF

BURGUNDY

CERISE

CERULEAN

CHAMOIS (pron. shammy)

CITRON

CLARET

COCOA

CORDOVAN

CRIMSON

DOVE

EBONY

ECRU

EMERALD

FUCHSIA

GRANITE

GRAY/GREY

GREEN

GREIGE

HAZEL

HENNA

HYACINTH

INDIGO

IVORY

JADE

LAVENDER

LILAC

MAGENTA

MAHOGANY

MAIZE

MARIGOLD

MAUVE

MOSS

OLIVE

PINK	TEAL
POPPY	TITIAN
	TOPAZ
RAVEN	TURQUOISE
RED	
ROAN	UMBER
ROSE	
ROSY	VERMILION
RUBY	VIOLET
RUSSET	VIRIDIAN
SCARLET	WISTERIA
SIENNA	
SILVER	XANTHENE
SLATE	
STEEL	ZINC
STERLING	

COOLEST
BIBLICAL NAME
• • •
Salome

Sonata

Music Names

If it's true that music 'has charms to soothe a savage breast' and is 'the food of love', then it stands to reason that the words used to describe music would be charming and soothing, lyrical, rhythmic and rousing. Some of them could even make melodious baby names:

ADAGIO	BRIO
ALLEGRO	
ALTO	CADENCE
ARABESQUE	CADENZA
ARIA	CALLIOPE

CALYPSO	MADRIGAL
CANTATA	MALAGUENA
CAPPELLA	MANDOLIN
CAPRICE	MARIMBA
CARILLON	MELODY
CELLO	MINUET
CLARION	
	OPERA
DIVA	
DULCIMER	RAGA
	REED
ÉTUDE	RHYTHM
FIFER	SERAPHINE
FLAMENCO	SERENADE
	SONATA
HARMONY	SONATINA
HARP	SYMPHONY
JAZZ	TANGO
	TEMPO
LUTE	TIMPANI
LYRE	
LYRIC	VIOLA

Jupiter

Space Names

There are cool celebrity star names like Uma and Bono, and then there are the even more extreme astronomical star and constellation names, which might appeal to parents looking for something truly unique and celestial – in other words, a heavenly name. Some stellar ideas:

ADHARA	ALULA
ALCYONE	ALYA
ALIOTH	AMALTHEA
ALTAIR	ANDROMEDA

AQUILA	JANUS
ARA	JUPITER
ARIES	
ASCELLA	LEDA
ATLAS	LIBRA
ATRIA	LUNA
AURORA	
AZHA	MAIA
	MARS
BELLATRIX	MEISSA
	MERCURY
CAELUM	METEOR
CALLISTO	MIMOSA
CALYPSO	MIRA
CAPELLA	MOON
CASSIOPEIA	
CHARA	NASHIRA
COLUMBA	NAVI
	NOVA
ELARA	
ELECTRA	OBERON
	ORION
GALATEA	
	PERSEUS
HALLEY	
IO	RHEA
IZAR	

SABIK   TITANIA
SHAULA
STAR   VEGA
STELLA   VENUS

TALITHA   ZANIAH
THALASSA   ZOSMA

Early

Beyond-name Names

I n our book *Beyond Jennifer & Jason, Madison & Montana*, we included vast numbers of 'word' names, nature names, day names, and surname-names. While these names are, for the most part, undoubtedly cool, there are an uncountable number of them, beyond the scope of any one book. The only limits are your reference books, your imagination and your taste. If you'd like to explore this territory further on your own, we can direct you to *B J & J, M & M* as well as to your dictionary, field guide and phone book. To give you an idea of some of the selections from these categories, we offer here a few of the best:

AFTERNOON

ARBOUR

BAY

BEECH

BIRCH

BOGART

CABOT

CAMEO

CANYON

CHRISTMAS

CLARITY

DECEMBER

EARLY

EASTER

EDISON

FINCH

GRAYSON

GROVE

HALE

JUNIPER

KEATON

LANE

LARK

LINCOLN

MADIGAN

MONDAY

NORTH

NOVEMBER

PIKE

QUARRY

SALMON

SEASON

SONNET

TIERNEY

Kool

Too-cool Names

Maybe you can't be too rich or too thin, but if you're a name, it just may be possible to be too cool.

What makes a name too cool? Trying so hard that coolness is its main – and maybe its only – merit. Being so aggressively hip that poor little Kool will bend under the expectations of grooviness created by his name. Sure, there are kids named Babe or Scorpio who grow into their names' images, but you're asking a lot of a child who, let's face it, is just as likely to have crooked teeth and a shyness issue as an awesome bod.

While the line of what constitutes a too-cool name seems to get redrawn every day, these choices will probably be on the wrong side of it for a long time to come:

ARMANI	MAVERICK
BABE	PORSCHE
BRANDY	PRINCE
BREEZE	
BUCK	RAMBO
	RIDER
CALIFORNIA	
CHEYENNE	SCORPIO
CONGO	SINBAD
CROCKETT	SUGAR
DESIRÉE	TALON
DUKE	THOR
	TIGER
FREE	
	VICE
HARLEY	VULCAN
KOOL	WILD

COOLEST
HERO NAME
• • •
Rudy

INDEX

68, 70, 101, 110, 114, 140, 144

Anais, Anaïs, 64, 93

Anastacia, Anastasia, 48, 52, 114, 121, 125, 137

Anatoli, 18

Andorra, 25

André, Andrea, Andreas, Andrew, Drew, 18, 42, 46, 52, 56, 63, 112, 134, 136–7

Andromeda, 9, 159

Anemone, 29

Ange, Angel, Angelica, Angelina, Angelo, Angelou, Anja, Anjelica, 17, 23, 29, 52, 73, 93, 137, 140, 153

Angus, 7, 42, 46

Anika, 17

Aniline, 155

Ansel, Anselm, Anselmo, 18, 80, 115

Answer, 153

Antarctica, 25

Anthony, Antoinette, Anton, Antonella, Antonia, Antonio, 17, 36, 48, 68, 77, 95, 121, 125, 135

Aoi, 61

Aoibhe, 5

Aoife, 5

Aphra, 93, 110

Aphrodite, 28

apl.d.apl, 138

Apollo, Apollonia, Apollos, 36, 112, 114

Apphia, Apphiah, 110

Apple, 63–4

Aqua, 155

Aquila, Aquilia, Aquilina, 110, 114, 144, 160

Aquitaine, 25

Ara, Arabella, Arabesque, Arabia, 25, 40, 93, 119, 157, 160

Aragon, 25

Araminta, 137

Arbor, 163

Arc, Arcadia, 61, 153

Archer, Archibald, Archie, 5, 32, 42, 99, 120

Ardesia, 144

Aretha, 86

Aria, Arria, 13, 110, 144, 157

Ariadne, 95

Ariel, Ariela, 17, 29

Aries, 160

Arjan, 103

Arley, Arlo, xi, 36, 86, 135, 137

Armando, Armani, 18, 36, 165

Armel, 23

Armstrong, 86, 103

Arne, Arno, Arnold, 10, 36, 128

Aro, 148

Arpad, 80

Arrecina, 110

Art, Artemas, Arthur, 23, 34, 80, 123

Arwen, 56

Asa, Asahel, Azha, 160

Ascella, 160

Ash, Ashe, Asher, Ashley, Ashlyn, Ashton, xi, 7, 10, 13, 45, 52, 59, 61, 103, 136, 155

Ashanti, 52, 86

Asia, Assia, 28, 121

Aspen, 25

Assisi, Assia, 23, 25, 65

Atarah, 110

Athalia, 110

Atlanta, Atlantique, Atlantis, Atlas, 25, 65, 140, 160

Atria, 160

Atticus, 99, 112

Aubrey, 13, 115

Auburn, 155

Auden, 65, 80, 91

Audra, Audrey, 22, 40, 51-2, 56, 80, 86

August, Augusta, Augustine, Augustus, 42, 46, 93, 112, 119, 125

Aurelia, Aurélien, Aurelius, Auretta, 65, 80, 110, 112, 144

Auric, 99

Aurora, 9, 96, 144, 148, 160

Austen, Austin, 93, 103

Autry, 32

Autumn, 13

Ava, 4, 7, 9, 40, 51, 65, 74

Avalon, Avelina, Aveline, Avellana, 17, 25, 119, 148

Avery, 13

Avitia, 110

Avril, 52, 86

Axel, Axelle, Axl, 86, 100

Ayn, 91, 101

Azekan, 117

Aziza, 17, 138

Azrael, 56

Azubah, 114

Azure, 154–5

Azzedine, 81

Babe, 164–5

Bacca, 144

Baez, 87

Bai, Baia, Bay, Baya, 29, 144, 148, 163

Bailey, 135

Baldwin, xi, 93

Balia, 144

Ballard, 93

Balthasar, Balthazar, 42, 52

Balzo, 144

Banjo, 61, 65

Bannister, 104

Baptiste, 18

Barbara, 96–7, 114

Barley, 100

Barnabas, Barnaby, Barney, 32, 42, 100, 135

Barry, 123

Bartholomew, Bartleby, 56

Barzillai, 115

Bas, Basia, 45, 87

Basil, Basilia, Baz, Bazel, 42, 72, 110, 115

Bathsheba, 28, 96

Bea, Beata, Beatrice, Beatrix, 21, 31, 48, 66, 110, 118, 125

Beale, 100

Becan, 115

Bechet, Bechette, 87, 140

Beck, Becker, Beckett, Beckham, 52, 66, 87, 93, 104

Beech, 163

Behan, 93

Beige, 155

Bella, Bellatrix, Belle, Bellezza, Bellow, 40, 66, 78, 93, 144, 160

Ben, Benjamin, Bennato, Benno, Benson, Benvolio, 22, 23, 36, 45, 56, 100, 115, 144

Benajah, Benatar, 87

Benecio, Benet, Benicia, Benicio, 17, 36, 52, 93, 115

Castor, 56
Cat, Cate, Catherine, Catt, Kai, Kaia, Kat, Katarina, Kate, Katharine, Katya, Kay, 15, 17, 44–6, 52, 57–9, 67, 72, 81, 88, 104, 126
Catalina, 25, 96
Cathal, 6
Cato, 36, 100, 112
Catriona, 96
Cayenne, 28
Cayman, 25
Ceara, 114
Cecil, Cecily, Cicely, 40, 67, 81, 114, 119, 124
Cedro, 149
Cellini, Cello, 83, 158
Cerise, 155
Cerulean, 155
Cesaria, 110
Ceylon, 25
Chaka, 52, 56, 87
Chamois, 155
Chan, Chance, Chandler, Chanel, Chantal, 13, 17, 45, 83, 93, 100, 153
Chara, Chardin, Charity, Charmian, Charra, 29, 83, 96, 149, 160
Chase, Chasen, Chastity, 29, 56, 136
Chaton, 140
Chauncey, 110
Cheever, 93
Cher, x, 154
Cheyenne, Shyanne, 13, 165
Chiara, 23
Chili, 56
China, 52
Chirico, Chi, 75, 83
Chloe, ix
Christanel, Christian, Christianson, Christmas, Christo, Crisli, Crispin, Crispina, Cristabelle, Cristian, Cristobal, Crystal, Kristof, Krizia, 19, 42, 56, 83–4, 110, 135, 163
Cia, Cinda, Cindy, Cynthia, Sidda, Siddalee, Sidney, Sidony, Sidra, Sydney, 7, 9, 18, 45, 99, 123–4
Cian, Kian, 6

Ciarran, 6
Cicero, 36
Cielo, 145, 149
Cilla, Cillian, Cillinan, Killian, 6, 52, 137
Cisco, Sisqo, 56, 91
Citron, 155
Claes, 83
Claire, Clara, Claret, Clarice, Clarion, Clarissa, Clarity, 23, 29, 40, 96, 125, 134, 155, 158, 163
Claudia, Claudine, Claudio, Claudius, 36, 40, 79, 112, 119, 125
Clay, Clayton, Clea, 14, 42, 52, 96
Clea, 23
Clem, Clemencia, Clemens, Clement, Clemente, Clementine, 22, 23, 40, 45, 70, 80, 100, 110, 115
Cleo, Cleon, 28, 36, 100
Clerick, 56
Clete, 115
Clips, 91
Clodagh, 5
Cloud, 61
Clove, Clover, 40, 56
Cluny, 25
Coco, Cocoa, 28, 31, 67–68, 83, 155
Cody, 14, 56, 100
Coe, 104
Colby, 14
Cole, Colette, Colin, Colina, Collin, 14, 42, 56, 58, 83, 87, 149
Colm, 6
Colomba, Colombia, Colorado, Columba, 25, 36, 110, 145, 160
Colton, Coltrane, 14, 87, 135
Comfort, 29
Common, 91
Conall, Conan, 115
Concha, 149
Congo, 165
Connemara, Connor, 25
Conrad, Conran, 83, 93
Constance, Constant, Constantin, Constantine, Consuelo, 29, 36, 119–21
Cooper, 7, 14, 33, 93, 104
Cora, 126

Corbett, Korben, Corbin, 14, 104
Cordelia, Cordovan, 119, 126, 155
Corentin, 18
Corin, 52, 100
Cormac, 42
Cornelia, Cornell, 83, 126, 137
Coro, Corot, 83, 145
Corry, 104
Corsica, 25
Cortesia, Cortez, 14, 149
Cosima, 17, 68
Cosmas, Cosmo, Coz, 36, 45, 112
Cotton, 56
Craig, Crispin, Crosby, 10, 42, 52, 115
Crane, 93
Crash, 61
Crespo, 104
Cressida, 40, 96
Crosby, 87
Cruz, 68
Crystal, 9
Cuba, 25, 52, 57
Currier, 83
Cy, Cyane, Cyprian, Cyprus, 25, 80, 83, 96, 115
Cylia, 23
Cyr, Cyra, Cyriac, Cyril, Cyrus, Siri, Sy'rai, 18, 57, 110, 112, 115, 124, 138

Dahlia, 96
Daire, 6
Daisy, 4, 9, 31, 40, 45, 68, 96, 118
Dakota, 14, 81
Dallin, 14
Dalton, 14, 135
Damaris, 110
Damian, Damiane, Damon, 11, 52, 110
Dana, Dane, 14, 58
Dania, Danica, Danilo, Danira, 13, 17, 36
Dante, Danton, 61, 93, 135
Danza, 145
Daphne, 40
Darcy, 100
Daria, Darius, Dashiell, 10, 114, 122
Darl, Darlo, 100, 135

Eoghan, 6
Eoin, 6
Ephraim, Ephram, 110, 115
Erasmo, Erasmus, 19, 115
Erwin, Erwan, 22, 23
Esau, 115
Esmé, 68, 96
Essence, 13
Estella, Ester, Esther, Estrella, 17, 29, 69–70, 126, 149
Ethan, Ethne, 7, 42, 57, 72, 135, 154
Ethel, Ethelbert, Ethereal, 109, 128, 153
Étienne, 19
Etta, 87
Étude, 158
Euan, Ewan, Ewing, 42, 69, 104
Eudora, 93, 101
Eugène, Eugenia, Eugenie, 40, 118, 119, 126, 128, 136
Eunice, 128
Euphemia, 119
Eustacia, 119
Eva, Evan, Evander, Evangeline, Evanna, 40, 52, 57, 97, 104
Eve, Evelyn, Evie, 9, 32, 40, 96, 101, 102, 114
Ever, Everest, Evert, Everly, 25, 87, 104, 153
Evonne, 104
Ewan, 5, 52
Ezekiel, Ezra, 42, 115, 137

Fabbro, Fabrique, Fabrizio, 87, 141, 145
Fabia, Fabian, Fabiola, 110, 114–15
Fable, 102
Faith, 29, 114
Faldo, 104
Famke, 52
Fannia, Fanny, 28, 110
Faro, 145
Farrah, 52
Faunia, 57, 97
Faustina, Fausto, 79, 122
Fay, Fè, 101, 126, 145
Feather, 97
Federica, 17, 21
Felicity, Felix, xi, 22, 29, 40, 42, 52, 115
Fenno, 100

Feodore, 119
Ferelith, 110
Fergus, 42
Fernanda, Fernando, 17, 36
Fia, Fiamma, 17, 145
Fiero, 145
Fifer, 158
Fifi, 28, 68
50 Cent, 91
Filippo, Phila, Phillida, Phillip, Philippa, Philippine, Philo, Philomon, Phyllis, Pip, Pippa, 21, 26, 37, 47–8, 97, 111, 128
Finch, Finlay, Finn, Finnian, Finnigan, xi, 5, 6, 42, 70, 115, 120, 163
Fiona, Fee, 40, 46, 58
Fiore, 145
Fisher, 14
Fitzgerald, Fitzwilliam, 93, 100
Flambeau, Flame, Flamenco, 28, 141, 158
Flann, Flannery, Flynn, 19, 93
Flavia, Flavie, 23, 110
Fleur, Fleurette, Flo, Flor, Flora, Florence, Florida, Flory, Flower, 23, 29, 32, 40, 46, 97, 126, 141, 149
Flynn, 7, 80
Ford, 83
Forest, Forrest, Forster, Fortune, 42, 74, 93, 153
Fraise, 141
France, Frances, Francesca, Francesco, Francis, Frangia, Frank, Franka, Frankie-Jean, Franklin, Franz, 17, 21, 29, 32, 40, 46, 81, 119, 126, 128, 145
Fraser, Frazier, 42, 104
Fred, Frederica, Fritz, Fritzi, 19, 32, 46
Free, Freesia, Frida, Frieda, 29, 57, 83, 128, 165
Freya, 40
Frisco, 36
Frost, 93, 105
Fyodor, Fyodora, 17, 19, 101

Gabe, Gabo, Gabriel, Gabriela, Gabriella,

Gabrielle, 40, 42, 53, 78, 83, 104, 115, 122, 135, 137
Gage, 15
Gaia, 70
Galán, Galatea, Galaxia, Galla, 110, 149, 160
Galette, 141
Galway, 25, 93
Gannon, 15
Garbo, Garcelle, Garcia, Garon, Garrett, Garth, Garvey, Gary, Gerhard, Guardian, 22, 87, 124, 135, 149, 153
Garfield, 104
Gaston, 19
Gauguin, 83
Gavin, Gaviota, 135, 149
Gay, Gaynor, 110, 128
Gaza, 117
Gehrig, Gehry, 83
Gelsey, Gèlso, 17, 145
Gemella, Gemma, Gèmma, Gena, Genesis, Geneva, Genevieve, Jeanette, Jem, Jemima, Jena, Jenna, Jennet, Jennifer, 9, 40, 46, 56–7, 87, 111, 114, 134, 145, 152–3
Genesis, 13
Geneva, Genevieve, 9
Geoff, 11
George, Georgette, Georgia, Georgina, Giorgia, Giorgio, 9, 21, 36, 40, 46, 57, 59, 83, 95–6, 98, 102
Geraint, 104
Gerda, Gershwin, Gertrud, Gertrude, Gervase, 22, 87, 98, 115, 128
Germain, Gerrit, Jeremiah, Jeremy, Jericho, Jerrick, Jersey, Jerzy, Jerusha, 26, 36, 57, 83, 94, 100, 114–15, 117, 135, 137
Giacomo, 11, 36
Giada, 145
Gianna, Gianni, 17, 19
Gide, Gideon, 93, 115
Gigi, 28, 68, 70
Gil, Gillespie, 87
Giles, 104, 115
Ginevra, 97
Gioia, 17
Giovanetta, Giovanni, 21, 57

· 176 ·

About the Authors

PAMELA REDMOND SATRAN is a contributing editor for *Parenting* magazine and a columnist for *Baby Talk*. Her first novel, *The Man I Should Have Married,* was published by Downtown Press/Pocket Books in March 2003. Satran's articles appear frequently in publications ranging from the *New York Times* to *Glamour* and *Self*. She lives outside New York City with her husband and three children.

LINDA ROSENKRANTZ is the author of seven other books in addition to the baby-naming series, ranging from *Gone Hollywood,* a social history of the film colony; to a childhood memoir, *My Life as a List: 207 Things About My (Bronx) Childhood;* to her latest book, a history and anthology of telegrams. A resident of Los Angeles, she also writes a syndicated weekly column on collectibles.

As authorities on baby names, they have been quoted in *People,* the *Wall Street Journal,* and the *New York Times Magazine*. They have also made appearances on nationally syndicated shows such as *Oprah* and the CNN Morning News. Their baby-name books have sold nearly one million copies.